Bringing
Catholic Youth
and the
Bible
Together

Editor: Brian Singer-Towns

Contributing Authors: Lisa-Marie Calderone-Stewart, Carole Goodwin, Joe Grant, Maryann Hakowski, Margaret Nutting Ralph, Bishop Richard J. Sklba, Tony Tamberino, Michael Theisen

 Genuine recycled paper with 10% post-consumer waste.
Printed with soy-based ink.

The publishing team included Brian Singer-Towns, development editor; Mary Duerson, copy editor; Barbara Bartelson, production editor; Hollace Storkel, typesetter; Cindi Ramm, art director; Cären Yang, designer; produced by the graphics division of Saint Mary's Press.

The quotation on pages 7–8 is from *New Directions in Youth Ministry: A National Study of Catholic Youth Ministry Program Participants,* by Bryan T. Froehle (Washington, DC: Center for Applied Research in the Apostolate, 1996), page 16. Copyright © 1996 by the National Conference of Catholic Bishops and the National Federation for Catholic Youth Ministry.
   The article by Bishop Sklba on pages 10–12 first appeared in the *Catholic Herald,* 16 December 1999.
   The scriptural quotation on pages 16–17 is from the New Revised Standard Version of the Bible. Copyright © 1989 by the Division of Christian Education of the National Council of the Churches of Christ in the United States of America, and is used by permission. All rights reserved.
   The scriptural quotations on page 50 are based on The Good News Bible, in Today's English Version. Copyright © 1966, 1971, 1976 by the American Bible Society.

Printed in the United States of America

Printing: 9 8 7 6 5 4 3 2 1

Year: 2008 07 06 05 04 03 02 01 00

ISBN 0-88489-692-7

Library of Congress Cataloging-in-Publication Data

Bringing Catholic youth and the Bible together : strategies and activities for parishes and schools / [general editor, Brian Singer-Towns; contributing authors, Lisa-Marie Calderone-Stewart . . . [et al.]].
   p. cm.
Includes bibliographical references.
ISBN 0-88489-692-7 (pbk.)
1. Bible—Study and teaching—Catholic Church. 2. Church group work with teenagers.
3. Catholic youth—Religious life. I. Singer-Towns, Brian. II. Calderone-Stewart, Lisa-Marie.
BS587.B75 2000
220'.071'2—dc21

                                                                00-010501

Contents

Activities

Introduction

The Challenge of Bringing
Catholic Youth and the Bible Together

*A*s a college student in the midseventies, I was part of an ecumenical Bible study. Born and raised Catholic, I attended Mass regularly growing up. I was even a lector in my small country parish as a teen. Yet I had not cracked open a Bible on my own more than two or three times. So my friends in the Bible study had to teach me some basic Bible skills such as how to locate specific passages and how to interpret particular Scripture teachings in light of the Bible's bigger themes.

In many respects you could say I was functionally biblically illiterate. Of even greater concern was my lack of biblically based faith and values. Despite my participation in the Eucharist week after week, I still held the materialistic and self-absorbed values of popular culture. It was my involvement in the Bible study group and my own personal reading of the Scriptures that became the catalyst for a personal conversion to a Gospel-centered spirituality.

Biblical literacy among Catholic youth today isn't much different from my experience of twenty-five years ago. Most Catholic teens cannot name the four Gospels. In a Gallup study in the early 1990s, only 20 percent of Catholic youth, compared with 60 percent of Christian youth from other denominations, claimed to have ever read the Bible on their own.

This is a major evangelization and catechetical challenge for the Catholic community. Those of us ministering to Catholic youth must become more intentional in fostering biblical literacy and biblical spirituality. We are supported in this goal by the Catholic bishops and the National Federation for Catholic Youth Ministry (NFCYM). A Center for Applied Research in the Apostolate (CARA) study, which was sponsored by the bishops and the NFCYM, has this major recommendation: "Catholic youth ministry needs to be more persuasive in helping participants understand that reading the

Bible is important for growing in their faith" (Froehle, *New Directions in Youth Ministry,* page 16).

If you read it carefully, this recommendation makes it clear that getting young people to read the Bible is not enough. Helping teens to use the Bible to grow in their faith is also necessary. We must encourage students to pray with the Bible and to live out the Bible's values. This holistic approach is captured in the Saint Mary's Press "Pray It, Study It, Live It" Scripture motto. Just as with adults, teens' minds, hearts, and wills are organically connected. We must find ways to touch our young people's hearts and wills with God's word as well as educating their minds about it.

We have two goals, then, if we hope to meet the challenge of bringing Catholic youth and the Bible together. The first is developing biblical literacy in our teens. And the second is helping them foster a biblical spirituality. Accomplishing these goals may require some changes in how we use the Scriptures with young people. For instance, rather than have them read about the Bible in some other book, we must challenge them to plunge into the Bible itself. Rather than teach them what the Bible says, we must help them discover on their own what the Bible teaches. Rather than use the Bible solely as a proof text, we must help them to see the Bible as a living text that can change their life.

Saint Mary's Press has made a commitment to provide resources and services to help respond to these goals. We want to help young Catholics pray the Bible, study the Bible, and live the Bible's values and teachings. We believe that by working together with teachers, coordinators of youth ministry, directors of religious education, catechists, and other youth ministry volunteers, we can significantly increase biblical literacy and biblical spirituality among Catholic youth.

In this book youth ministry and catechetical leaders present background and activities for developing biblical literacy and fostering biblical spirituality. The chapters by Bishop Sklba and Margaret Nutting Ralph provide important background on how Catholics approach and interpret the Scriptures. Carole Goodwin and Joe Grant share how the Bible can be a compass for our ministry with young people. Lisa-Marie Calderone-Stewart shows how to use the ancient prayer form of *lectio divina* with teens. I offer a model for understanding biblical literacy and activities for teaching it. Maryann Hakowski and Tony Tamberino offer a variety of activities for making the people and teachings of the Bible come alive. Michael Theisen provides a fun approach to learning about the Scriptures under the guise of a game show.

The ideas and activities in this book can be used in whatever ministry you have with young people. Keep it handy and refer to it often. Share it with other people in your school or parish who work with youth. Let it spark your own imagination for using the Bible with teens. Listen and learn from others. Be particularly attentive to youth ministers from other Christian denominations whose practical experience in using the Bible with youth often surpasses our own. And most important, let us listen to the Spirit speaking through our young people. Bringing Catholic youth and the Bible together—we can do it!

In the words of Saint Paul, grace and peace!

Brian Singer-Towns
Editor

Reading the Scriptures
as a Catholic

Bishop Richard J. Sklba

This brief chapter is taken from a talk that Bishop Sklba delivered to the 1999 National Catholic Youth Congress. Bishop Sklba reflects on the attitudes that Catholics bring to Scripture study and prayer. These attitudes distinguish us from some fundamentalist Christian approaches to the Scriptures. Bishop Sklba's insights provide a solid foundation for teaching the young people we work with about the Catholic approach to the Scriptures.

*L*ike all other Christians, we Catholics bring our faith to everything we do, namely, the basic conviction that Jesus is the risen Lord, who shares his Spirit with his disciples through Baptism and continues to send us forth to proclaim the Good News. In opening the pages of the Scriptures, we believe that God has chosen a people and guided them through the centuries. As believers, we find biblical witness to all the ways God has loved his people into goodness.

As human beings blessed with intellectual gifts of understanding, imagination, and curiosity, we Catholics, like our Protestant neighbors, also read the Scriptures with eyes, heads, and hearts wide open. We look for everything, somewhat the way a person might read a letter from a distant friend or fiancée, searching for any clue or signal of how things are going.

But besides those attitudes common to most other Christians, we Catholics bring some special perspectives to private Bible study or prayerful use of the Scriptures. Allow me to list a few for the record:

As Catholics we know that the church has placed the Scriptures in our hands. By that I mean that the early Christian community selected those writings believed to be inspired by God. Successive generations carefully monitored the faithful transmission of these works and their translation over the centuries.

On the copyright page, a small cross with the word *imprimatur* and the name of an individual bishop signals the church's formal approval of the faithfulness of the translation we have in hand. Look for it when buying a Bible for someone. It is Catholic to be conscious of the way the church takes responsibility for bringing the word to us.

We Catholics pay special attention to the verbs. Perhaps you never thought about it, but the name of Israel's God is a verb, namely, YHWH (probably meaning, "he will make happen," or "he will call into existence"), and indeed the name of Jesus means, "he will save." Moreover, we regularly recite the creed's list of all God's activities—creating, choosing, loving, redeeming, saving, feeding, healing, and so on.

We expect that our Sunday Eucharist will inspire and energize the rest of the week's work. As a people we sense an obligation to open our lives to God's grace, and to be God's living instruments in shaping a more just and generous world. We are people on the move! Granted, we can do nothing without God's grace, but we are inclined toward activity, so we keep checking out the verbs.

We Catholics look for the "us" in everything. Virtually all the books of the Scriptures were intended to be heard and read by an entire community at prayer. We first heard them at Mass. Almost every time the word *you* occurs, it's actually a plural and probably should be translated "you all" in the manner of our southern friends.

Presume that the text is aimed at the entire community, and only afterward see what it might say to the individual reader. In a similar manner, we always pray, "Our Father," even when we're alone, because we have a strong social sense of community.

We Catholics are always mindful of the different ways of saying things. We believe that God chose to take all human speech, except error, in addressing us. Poetry expresses truth differently than a historical account. A proverb is yet another form of telling the truth about human nature.

Catholics, especially since the teachings of Pius XII, are always reminded to be conscious of the larger picture of each unit and are never satisfied with a phrase or sentence taken out of context. We look for the literary "forms" that surround every phase or story.

We Catholics keep looking for the history of things. We know that every biblical concept or practice has an original context within which it was established, and for which it was intended. When circumstances changed, it made a difference. Things developed. Precisely because we have such a constant sense of history, we stand before the Scriptures as if they were a three-paneled mirror in a clothing store, and we see our church community projected repeatedly into past and future ages.

Finally, we Catholics say, "Thank you." We always move from listening to the word of God to a solemn prayer of thanksgiving at the Eucharist, joining our voices to Christ's prayer of thanks and praise to his heavenly Father.

Similarly, every private prayer with the Scriptures should lead us into a prayer of gratitude for all the blessings of life, even those that may seem tough to handle at times. We are grateful people, and we can't stop saying a word of gratitude to the God of our lives.

These are some of the distinctive attitudes we bring to biblical prayer as Catholics. Make them your own, and experience the grace and joy of God's Word.

Bishop Sklba is the auxiliary bishop for the Archdiocese of Milwaukee. He has authored several books and articles on the Scriptures and has served on many different committees of the National Conference of Catholic Bishops. He is currently the chair of the ad hoc committee for reviewing Scripture translations.

What the Scriptures Say . . . and Don't Say

Margaret Nutting Ralph

In this chapter Margaret Nutting Ralph explores the connection between our approach to interpreting the Bible and God's revealed truth. She emphasizes that a critical factor for correctly understanding biblical truth is exploring the complete context of a particular book or passage. Margaret's insights will help us and the young people we work with avoid common misinterpretations of the Bible's teaching.

Have you ever heard two people who totally disagree with each other use Scripture to "prove" that God is on their side? Instead of letting the Scriptures form their thinking, they use a quote from the Scriptures, often taken out of context, to support their own opinions.

We've probably all done this to some extent. Even expert theologians use Scripture quotes to show that their teaching is rooted in the Bible. But a proper understanding of biblical revelation will challenge us to examine our approach to the Scriptures and overcome any tendency to quote the Bible out of context.

Instead of asking, "Do these words support what I already think?" we need to ask, "What is this passage trying to teach me?" When we recognize what the inspired biblical authors intend to teach, we are opening our minds and hearts to the revelation of the Scriptures.

The revealed Scriptures do not necessarily hold the same meaning we may want to attach to the words. The inspired biblical authors intended to say and teach certain truths, and we need to root our understanding of the Scriptures first and foremost in the intent of the author.

But how do we determine the intentions of an author who lived thousands of years ago in a totally different cultural setting? The church teaches us that in order to understand the revelation the Bible contains, we must learn first and foremost to read passages in the context in which they appear.

What are you reading? One way to safeguard against misunderstanding the intent of an author is to determine the kind of writing the author has chosen to use. Any piece of writing has a particular literary form: poetry, prose, fiction, essay, letter, historical account, and so on. This is as true of the biblical books as of any piece of contemporary writing.

If we misunderstand an author's literary form, we will misunderstand what the author intends to say. In order to understand what we are reading, then, we have to make allowances for the form and change our expectations accordingly.

We do this any time we read a newspaper, for example. As we turn the pages of a newspaper, we encounter a variety of literary forms—news, features, editorials, and so on—and we adjust our idea of what we can expect from the writing for each form.

For instance, after I read a news story, I expect to have the answer to the question What happened? I expect the author of a news story to be objective and evenhanded, to inform me of the facts. If the story is about something controversial, I expect the writer to cover all sides fairly.

When I get to the editorial page, I change my expectations. Now I know that the author is allowed to be persuasive rather than objective. I may find facts that support the author's point of view but nothing that contradicts that point of view.

So if I read an editorial with the same frame of mind with which I read a front-page news story, thinking that the author has responded to the question What happened? I will be misinformed after I finish my reading. It is not the author's fault that I am misinformed. It is my own.

How the inspired author tells the tale. Now let's look at how literary form functions in the Bible. One of the inspired biblical authors—the author of the Book of Job—has written in the form of a debate. This literary form demands that you be as persuasive as possible on both sides of an issue. If you write persuasively on the side you agree with and poorly on the side you disagree with, you have not written a good debate.

The author of the Book of Job lived at a time when people believed that all suffering was punishment for sin. He wrote a debate to argue against this belief. The author places his debate in the context of a pre-existing legend that establishes at the outset the fact that Job is innocent. So why is he suffering?

The author portrays Job's friends arguing with Job over the cause of his suffering. All the friends think that Job must have sinned or he wouldn't be suffering. They do not know, as does the audience, that Job's sinfulness is not the source of his suffering. The friends are wrong.

Now if you did not know that the Book of Job is a debate, in which some of the characters argue persuasively for the point of view with which the author disagrees, you might read an isolated passage and conclude that the book teaches the opposite of what the author intended to teach. You might think that the friends are teaching a valid message about suffering.

If we look at the book as a whole, we discover that the author places the truth he is teaching not on the lips of Job's friends but on the lips of God. God appears at the end of the debate and responds to the friends' arguments. Obviously, the author agrees with what God has to say. God contradicts the belief that all suffering is punishment for sin.

Because this book is in the canon, we know that it teaches revealed truth. We can only discover this revealed truth, however, if we look at the literary form of the book.

We need to remember, too, that the Bible is actually a "library" of many different books. To say that Job is a debate is not to say that the Bible as a whole is a debate or that a Gospel is a debate or that the Book of Revelation is a debate. The answer to the question What literary form am I reading? will vary from book to book. Often the introduction to each book in a good study Bible will give you the relevant literary form.

Culture in context. We have seen how easy it is to "misquote" the Bible by taking passages out of the context of their literary form. A second context we need to consider is the culture and the beliefs in place when the book was written. The inspired author and the original audience shared knowledge, presumptions, expressions, and concerns that may not be part of our awareness, but may nevertheless influence the meaning of the book or passage.

The inspired author may have applied the revealed message contained in a particular book to a shared cultural setting in order to make the message clearer. People sometimes mistake such applications for the heart of the revealed message. Thus they put the full authority of the Scriptures behind passages that reflect beliefs of the time rather than the unchanging truth the author intended to teach.

In expressing the revealed truth, a biblical author may show cultural biases and presumptions that later generations know are inaccurate. This kind of misunderstanding resulted in Galileo's excommunication. We know, as biblical authors did not, that the earth is not the center of the universe or even our solar system. We also know that the Bible does not claim to teach astronomy. Rather, the Bible addresses questions about the relationship between God and God's people, about what we should be doing to build up God's Kingdom rather than to tear it down.

A biblical author may also apply an eternal truth to a setting that is important to the original audience but not to us. For example, one of Paul's key insights is that the way we treat every other person is the way we treat the risen Christ. He applies this insight to the social order of his own day, an order that included slavery. We misuse the Scriptures if we say this application shows that God's social order includes slavery. While Paul's core message is eternally true revelation, the application was relevant only in its own cultural context.

Revelation is ongoing. A third context we must be aware of is the place the inspired author's insights have in the process of revelation. The Bible is not a book of bottom-line answers like a catechism.

The Bible is a "library of books" written over a two-thousand-year period. It reflects the process by which the inspired authors came to greater knowledge of God's revealed truth. People who do not realize or do not believe that the Bible reflects this progression take an early insight as the whole truth.

For example, people may make this mistake when arguing over the death penalty. Some people who support the death penalty try to put God's authority behind their opinion by quoting Scripture: An eye for an eye, a tooth for a tooth, a life for a life.

It is true that the Scriptures teach this (see Exod. 21:23–24). However, the teaching dates to the time of Exodus, about 1250 B.C. At the time, this teaching was an ethical step forward. It taught people not to seek escalating revenge: If you harm me, I can't do worse to you than you originally did to me.

Jesus later challenged people to grow beyond this teaching. He said, "You have heard that it was said, 'An eye for an eye and a tooth for a tooth.' But I say to you, . . . Love your enemies and pray for those who persecute you" (Matt. 5:38–44). Jesus did not say that the law was wrong, only that it did not go far enough. Jesus is the fulfillment of the law.

We are misusing the Scriptures if we quote Exodus to support the death penalty and fail to quote the words of Jesus in the Gospels. When we use a passage from the Scriptures to support our side of an argument, we must ask ourselves if the passage reflects the fullness of truth or whether it is a partial truth, perhaps an early insight.

Context, context, context. It is distressing to hear Christians abuse the Bible by quoting it in favor of unchristian positions. It is doubly distressing to realize that we ourselves might be guilty of this.

One way to avoid this mistake is to remember always to consider the context. Determine the place of a passage in its larger context. Ask yourself what literary form the author is using. Explore the beliefs and presumptions the author may share with the original audience. Learn something about the time when the book was written. Know how the author's insights fit into the process of revelation.

If we do this, we will avoid many a harmful error. We will be less likely to abuse the Scriptures and more likely to hear the revelation of God's love that the biblical authors intend us to hear.

Finally, invite the Holy Spirit to open up your mind and heart as you listen to the Word. Discerning God's will in your life will leave you with Christ's own peace in your heart.

Margaret Nutting Ralph is secretary for educational ministries for the Diocese of Lexington, Kentucky, and director of the master's degree programs for Roman Catholics at Lexington Theological Seminary. She has taught the Scriptures to high school students, college students, and adult education groups for twenty years. She is the author of the book and video "*And God Said What?*" and the Discovering the Living Word series (all from Paulist Press).

Making the Scriptures Your Youth Ministry Compass

Carole Goodwin and Joseph Grant

In this chapter Carole Goodwin and Joseph Grant make a case for integrating the Scriptures into all aspects of youth ministry and religious education. They encourage teachers and ministers to grow in their own use of the Scriptures, and they include some practical suggestions for when and how to use the Bible with young people.

Most ministers and teachers face some common questions in their work with teens:

- How do we help young people live happy, healthy, and holy lives?
- What topics, issues, and concerns should we be talking about with youth?
- How can we reach out to youth who are loosely connected, or not connected at all, to our group or class?
- How can we offer healing and hope to suffering teens?
- What do we say to kids in trouble?
- How do we pray with young people?
- What does God need from me to best serve the youth in my life?

We can respond to these questions in many ways. We look to seasoned ministers and teachers to mentor us. We investigate the popular culture to help set our agenda. We consult the many resources available to help in our planning. We learn from our experiences of teaching and ministering with youth. And of course we look to the Word of God, which has been the source of inspiration, direction, and challenge for our church for two thousand years. But how effective have we been in using the Scriptures with teens?

By and large, Catholic ministers and teachers use the Scriptures with youth in a limited and one-dimensional way. We have relied on it primarily as a kind of encyclopedia for kids to look up and verify something we are trying to get across. Nothing is necessarily wrong with this (except teaching that the Bible is primarily a proof text), but the Scriptures should be so much more in our life. It is a primary source to inspire, strengthen, and challenge us in living as Christ's disciples. We may resort to the more limited use, though, because we may not feel knowledgeable about the Bible or adequately prepared to teach it to others.

Take heart, people of God! We live in a wonderful moment of opportunity. Adults and young people alike are hungering for a deeper experience with the Word. The years since the Second Vatican Council have seen an explosion of resources and programs for making the Scriptures accessible to all people. So let us look first at how the Scriptures can be the compass that guides our life. Then let us look at how we can help young people make it the guide for their life.

The Compass for Your Life

The Word of God is a metaphor that calls to mind God's breath. God's breath gave life to all creation; the Word of God, the Scriptures, brings us to fullness of life. In the beginning was the Word and the Word became a part of us. All this is intimately connected to the work of the Holy Spirit. The spirit of God was with God in creation, inspired the sacred words of the Bible, and dwells within each one of us.

Thus, when we study and pray with the Bible, God's spirit within us is nurtured by the Spirit-inspired words of the Scriptures. Our spiritual and moral compass is renewed and strengthened. Our choices often become clearer, and even when they do not, we are given the patience and strength to endure the difficulties and ambiguities of life. This is not fantasy but the experience of countless generations of believers.

It is easy to be intimidated by the Scriptures because they will never be fully understood or grasped. But this must not become an excuse for not spending time with God's Word. Rely on the Holy Spirit to guide you. Sincerity and openness, honest questions, and faithful searching will allow God to speak through the stories of the Scriptures. It takes attention, time, silence, and care. Here are some simple suggestions for developing your relationship with the Scriptures.

Spend Time with the Word

Make the Bible your traveling companion. Pick it up with ease. Go to it first when faced with a problem or a difficulty. Use the daily or Sunday readings from the lectionary cycle as a source for your own prayer. Or read through a Gospel or another Bible book over a given period of time. As you read and pray, keep a journal of your insights and your questions. With the Scriptures, as with faith, the questions are more important than the answers. Invite the young people to question and reflect with you.

A simple process for unlocking the powerful Word of God is to probe a passage with the following questions:
- Is there a word about God in this passage?
- Is there a word from God for me?
- Is there a word from God for God's people?

You should also consider learning and practicing the simple but powerful technique of *lectio divina* described in the chapter "Teaching *Lectio Divina* to Young People." Knowing several ways of approaching the Scriptures can help renew your interest when your time with God's Word becomes dry and lifeless.

Become Bible Smart

Many wonderful resources are available to enhance your knowledge of the Bible. Start by studying the book introductions, glossary, indexes, maps, and notes included with most youth and study Bibles. Continue developing your biblical awareness by browsing commentaries and acquiring your own resources on the Scriptures for prayer and study. See appendix B, "Recommended Bible Resources," for a helpful list of some of the resources available. Also consider taking an introductory class or course in the Scriptures, if one is available in your area. Many Catholic colleges and diocesan formation programs offer such courses.

Break Open the Word with Others

Perhaps you have already been part of a group that used the Bible as a basis for sharing and discussion. Such sharing focuses less on the academic study of the Scriptures and more on the connection between the Bible's stories and our stories. Breaking open God's Word with others in this way has the power to make God's Word alive in our life. Many people find this to be an essential part of their spiritual life.

You do not have to start or join a group to make such sharing a part of your life. Perhaps you could work it into other meetings you already have, such as teacher meetings or activity planning sessions. The other people you gather with may appreciate the opportunity as much as you.

Decorate Your Life with Sacred Words

Surrounding yourself with biblical quotes and images is a subtle way for deepening the inspiration the Scriptures has in your life. When you find a meaningful passage from the Scriptures, rewrite it on paper, a card, or poster board and put it somewhere where you will see it regularly, decorating your life, home, office, and youth room.

The Compass for Young People

In ministry we often are tempted to pick the fast, easy road to programming, to reach for the resources on the shelf in preparing for a project, class, or youth gathering. At times the lyric of a popular song gives rise to a great retreat theme. We choose our hot topics from a list of discussion-starters, or we opt for the guaranteed crowd-breaker activities to get the teens fired up.

These are all good techniques in our ministry and teaching with young people. But when they are used exclusively, they wear thin. Many young people and we ourselves want to move deeper into the heart of the Christian life. What is the stuff of this deeper experience? We believe that studying and praying the Scriptures with young people is certainly one of the elements to consider. We must help young people discover the revolutionary words of the Scriptures as a time-tested compass to guide their life.

A goal of youth ministry should be to integrate the Scriptures into every gathered moment with young people, turning to it first for direction, themes, and goals. This is perhaps at first not an easy practice, but it will become easier as we grow more comfortable with and knowledgeable about the Bible, and as new resources for using the Bible with Catholic youth become available.

Principles for Breaking Open the Word with Youth

Focus on making the Scriptures come *alive!* The Bible was not meant to be a coffee-table book. It is about our life today; it is not simply stories about the past. Through creative activities, reflection, questioning, and prayer, we can help young people see that God's Word helps us see the meaning of our life today. See Jesus' use of the Scriptures in the Emmaus story (Luke 24:13–35). See the remaining chapters for activities and techniques you can use.

Treat the Bible as a sacred story. Because the Bible is a sacred story, we should not reduce it to a school subject. The Bible emerged from the prayerful reflection of Jewish and early Christian communities on their experiences of God and Christ. We will come closest to its powerful messages when we engage young people in reflection and prayerful questioning on its texts and themes. This will require imagination and creativity, particularly from classroom teachers.

Find personal meaning in the Scriptures. If the Scriptures have personal importance to us, the adult ministers and teachers, our enthusiasm for God's Word will be passed on to the young people we work with. Reverencing, reading, reflecting on, and studying the Bible must be part of our own spiritual life.

Opportunities for Using the Bible with Youth

Be creative in integrating opportunities for using the Word of God into your ministry and teaching with teens.

When crafting retreats. Before selecting a theme for a retreat or planning retreat activities, turn first to the Scriptures for guidance. Use the readings of the liturgical season or invite youth to share favorite meaningful or challenging scriptural passages. The Scriptures should be highlighted as the major source for retreat planning.

At youth group meetings and planning sessions. Pray with the Scriptures and invite the Word of God to offer direction for youth gatherings, especially when you are discerning direction for the year or planning youth activities.

Before, during, and after service or outreach experiences. Frame outreach or service experiences with guiding words about God's call to justice and care for needy people. Make and distribute Scripture cards and invite the young people to carry the Word with them. Read the Scriptures aloud and pray with the group before engaging in service. Reflect on scriptural readings after challenging experiences of outreach. The words of the prophets (Isaiah, Micah, Joel, Jeremiah, etc.), as well as Jesus' admonitions to serve and care, are excellent resources for outreach reflection.

When offering pastoral care. Pastoral care always involves prayer. When young people come to share their problems, listen to a reading from the Scriptures together. Use passages of consolation or challenge. Or use the stories of Jesus forgiving and healing, which are excellent images for pastoral care.

Always during prayer. The Word of God represents the prayerful quests of our ancestors and has been used for millennia by Christians as they recognize the presence of God in their life. Use the Scriptures as often as possible in prayer—singing, reading together, listening, or rewriting the Psalms for young people.

Throughout sacramental preparation. Identify readings from the New Testament that illustrate the origins of our sacraments and find ways to dramatize, reflect on, and share these episodes.

During classroom sessions. Give the Word of God a central place during religious education or CCD classes by identifying key Scripture passages for each session. Find new ways to share the Word, such as guided meditation, dramatic reading, echo (or chorus) reading. Use appropriate games, discussions, and creative rewriting of the Scriptures to help bring to life the people and events of the Bible.

By treating the Bible with reverence. The book of God's Word has power as a symbol. Place the Bible in a position of prominence in your classroom, meeting room, or home. Treat it with reverence and open it daily. Place it on a bookstand or a covered table and set other religious symbols around it.

By creating your own liturgies of the Word and rituals for reading and sharing the Scriptures. Invite and train young people who are interested to share the Scriptures with their peers. Challenge the parish to occasionally offer a liturgy of the Word for teens on Sundays. Develop rituals and traditions in your youth gatherings that encourage young people to listen, pray, and live the Word.

By giving young people good and usable Bibles. High school seniors, retreat leaders, or youth council members can benefit from the gift of a solid and readable Bible. Give them as Confirmation gifts or as an affirmation of a young person's spiritual growth.

By making Scripture resources available. Use youth ministry funds (or fund-raising) to ensure that the youth room has a variety of different Bible translations as well as a commentary and concordance. Ensure that Catholic Bibles are readily accessible to young people.

By becoming familiar with the lectionary and its cycles. Use a lectionary guide or a calendar that identifies the readings of the day, Sunday, and season. Be attentive to the liturgical cycle and its scriptural messages. Resources such as lector handbooks and the series In Touch with the Word (Saint Mary's Press) can also be helpful.

By decorating your gathering areas with biblical quotes and images. Decorate your classrooms, halls, and meeting rooms with posters with Bible verses and images from Bible stories. Better yet, have the young people create their own posters using their favorite verses and stories. Be sure to update them from time to time. You will be creating an atmosphere supporting biblical literacy and biblical values.

Using these ideas as a starting point, the Scriptures can become an indispensable compass in your life and in the lives of the young people you work with.

Carole Goodwin is the director of youth ministry for the Archdiocese of Kentucky, and **Joseph Grant** is the consultant for youth ministry for the same archdiocese. Both have extensive experience in youth ministry and education. Carole is the author of two courses in the high school Horizons Program, and Joseph is the author of two books in the new HELP series, both from Saint Mary's Press.

Strategies for Teaching Biblical Literacy

Brian Singer-Towns

In this chapter Brian Singer-Towns explores what it means to be biblically literate and introduces his ABC's of biblical literacy. He also provides descriptions for a number of activities that can be used to develop biblical literacy in the young people you work with.

*I*n the introduction to this book, I mentioned how my involvement in an ecumenical Bible study in college forced me to learn some important skills for using the Bible. Over the course of that Bible study, the other participants began to notice an interesting phenomena. Despite my lack of skill in navigating the Scriptures, I was actually quite well versed in many of the biblical stories themselves. During our discussions I often said something like, "I don't know where it is, but this reminds of something else Jesus said." My friends were amazed that I could on the one hand be so ignorant in citing chapter and verse and on the other hand know so much of the Bible's stories and teaching.

This illustrates that when we talk about biblical literacy, we are talking about a spectrum of skills and knowledge. Like me, the young people you work with might be quite skilled in some areas of biblical knowledge and poorly skilled in other areas. I want to describe a simple formula describing biblical literacy that has helped me identify the biblical literacy needs of the young people that I minister to and with.

After that I will share some activities and strategies for addressing those needs.

The ABC's of Biblical Literacy

The formula I have developed is called the ABC's of biblical literacy. Each of the three letters stands for an important skill area for using and understanding the Bible. *A* stands for the skills needed to **a**ccess the stories and teachings of the Scriptures. *B* stands for the knowledge of the Bible's **b**ig picture. *C* stands for the ability to interpret a particular book or passage in its proper **c**ontext. Any person with knowledge and skills in all three areas can truly be called biblically literate. Let's look at each of these areas in closer detail.

Access

Biblically literate Catholic youth should have quick and easy access to the biblical text. They must be able to find a passage by themselves. They must be familiar with the names and general order of the Bible's books. They should know the major divisions of the Bible (the Pentateuch, the historical books, the wisdom and poetry books, the prophetic books, the Gospels and the Acts of the Apostles, and the letters and Revelation). This skill comes with repeated use of the Bible under the direction of an able teacher or mentor or even a biblically literate peer.

Thus, some objectives we should have in this skill area are as follows:
- to help the young people develop the ability to locate a passage in the Bible
- to help the young people know the names and order of the books in the Bible
- to teach the young people the major divisions of the biblical books

*B*ig Picture

To really appreciate the meaning of the individual books in the library that we call the Bible, a young person needs to be familiar with the overall biblical narrative, which we call salvation history. That history is generally divided into two parts, the stories of the Jewish people told in the Old Testament books and the stories of Jesus' life and ministry and the early church told in the New Testament books. These two parts are intimately connected so that to fully appreciate the New Testament, we must also be familiar with the Old Testament and vice versa.

To know how each biblical book's story fits into this bigger history is the mark of a truly biblically literate person. This familiarity does not come easily, but many resources and creative techniques exist to help teach it. It is a knowledge that grows with repetition and review. Some objectives we should have in this knowledge area are as follows:

- to help the young people become familiar with the major places, people, and events in the Bible
- to teach the young people the chronology and meaning of the major events in biblical history
- to help the young people understand the relationship between the Old and New Testaments of the Bible

Context

It is possible for a young person to have access to the biblical text and be familiar with the big picture of the biblical narrative but still misinterpret God's revelation in the Bible. Biblical fundamentalism is the prime example of such misinterpretation. Biblical fundamentalists often fail to put the Bible's stories and teachings in proper context. To help Catholic young people avoid biblical fundamentalism, we must teach them to ask the following contextual questions when reading any biblical book or passage:

- What is the literary genre of this book or passage?
- What historical or cultural situation was the author of this book or passage addressing?
- How does this story fit with the rest of the Bible's message or teaching?
- How does the church understand or interpret this book or passage?

Margaret Nutting Ralph's chapter in this book, "What the Scriptures Say . . . and Don't Say," is an excellent introduction to the contextual interpretation of the Scriptures. In order to help Catholic youth interpret the Bible contextually, we must work at the following objectives:

- to assist the youth in understanding the meaning of truth and inerrancy when applied to the Bible
- to familiarize the young people with the different literary genres found in the Bible
- to teach the young people the stages involved in the development of the Bible: the lived experience, the oral tradition, the writing and editing, and the formation of the canon

Activities

The following activities are among those that I use to help young people develop biblical literacy. Not every activity requires that each person have their own Bible, but it is good practice when promoting biblical literacy to encourage everyone to bring their own Bible to the meeting. There are many other ways to accomplish these objectives for biblical literacy. Please see the other chapters in this book for further ideas.

Bible Post-It Tabs

This activity helps young people identify the major sections of the Bible. It can be used with other activities designed to give an overview of the Bible (see the activities "Bible Bang" and "Bible Journey Simulation").

Skill areas. access, big picture

Age level. younger and older adolescents

Materials needed. two colors of small Post-it notes, enough so that each participant can have two of one color and four of the other; Bibles, one for each person

1. Make sure every participant has a Bible and six Post-it notes, two of one color and four of another. Have the young people locate and place the four Post-it notes of the same color on the first page of the following Old Testament books: Genesis, Joshua, Job, and Isaiah. Tell them to place the remaining two Post-it notes of the other color on the first page of the New Testament books of Matthew and Romans. Be sure they place the Post-it notes so that about one-fourth inch of the note protrudes from the long edge of the book.

2. Explain that the Post-it notes serve as tabs marking the six major sections of the Bible: the Pentateuch, the historical books, the wisdom and poetry books, the prophetic books, the Gospels and the Acts of the Apostles, and the letters and Revelation. As the young people place the tabs in front of each of the six sections, comment on the content of the books in that section. A good reference is *The Catholic Youth Bible* (Saint Mary's Press), which contains a two-page overview for each section.

Options

- Do this activity at the beginning of a unit or class on the Scriptures and keep the tabs in place for the duration of the unit or class.
- Write the name of each Bible section on the edge of the Post-it note tab to be placed at the beginning of that section.
- Instead of using Post-it tabs, allow the young people to color the page edges of each Bible section with a different colored marker, creating a rainbow effect.
- If the Bibles have a Bible timeline, match the historical period covered by each Bible section to the corresponding period on the timeline.

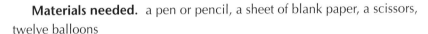

Skill area. access, big picture

Age level. younger adolescents

Materials needed. a pen or pencil, a sheet of blank paper, a scissors, twelve balloons

Before the activity. Copy the following list onto a blank sheet of paper and cut apart each line, making narrow slips of paper. Fold each slip of paper and insert it into a balloon, one slip for each balloon. Do not blow up the balloons. Hide the uninflated balloons throughout your meeting area or classroom.

1. Genesis 22:15–18 (Abraham's covenant)
2. Exodus 20:2–3 (first commandment)
3. 1 Samuel 12:13–15 (a king)
4. 2 Chronicles 36:15–17,20 (the Exile)
5. Psalm 100 (praising God)
6. Wisdom 6:22 (Lady Wisdom)
7. Isaiah 60:1–3 (God's promise)
8. Amos 1:4–6 (God's judgment)
9. Luke 1:30–33 (the Annunciation)
10. John 3:16–17 (salvation)
11. Galatians 3:26–29 (faith)
12. Revelation 22:12–13 (a new heaven)

1. Announce to everyone that you have found a treasure that can answer life's questions and help each one of them to live a happy, healthy, and holy life. Clues to finding that treasure are hidden throughout the room. It is their job to find the clues and discover how to use them. Give them permission to begin their search.

The young people should soon find the hidden balloons. They should discover that the balloons contain a clue. Encourage them to think of a creative (and noisy) way to retrieve the clues. They will soon figure out that to get the clues, they have to blow up and pop the balloons.

2. After all the clues have been recovered, ask the participants what they need to decode the clues. Of course the answer is the Bible. Pass out Bibles and have the young people look up the passage listed on each clue. Ask someone to read aloud each passage, starting with Genesis and proceeding in order through Revelation. After each passage is read, make a few comments on what it illustrates.

Options

- The passages listed in this activity are intended to give a brief overview of salvation history and the Bible's contents. Two passages are given for each of the six major sections of the Bible. You may wish to combine reading the passages with the activity "Bible Post-It Tabs" for increased retention.
- Choose your own passages to introduce a book of the Bible or a particular biblical theme.
- Use this activity for review by having the young people explain the meaning of the passages you hide within each balloon.

Bible Church Road Rally

Skill area. access

Age level. younger adolescents

Materials needed. pens or pencils; slips of paper; masking tape; a Bible concordance (optional); Bibles, one for each group; simple prizes

Before the activity. Create a list of Bible verses that contain the names of objects that can be found in your parish or school complex.

A sample list of verse possibilities and their corresponding objects follows. You can use a Bible concordance to find other verses that mention objects particular to your parish or school complex.

Attach to each object a slip of paper on which you have written the next verse citation on your list. When you come to the last object on your list, attach to it the slip for the first citation on your list. If more than one object in your parish or school complex fits a particular verse, pick the most well known or prominent one—unless you want to make this activity really difficult!

Verse	Object
1. Revelation 3:20	door
2. Genesis 8:20	altar
3. Galatians 6:14	cross
4. Acts of the Apostles 20:9	window
5. Psalm 119:105	lamp (light)
6. Zechariah 13:1	fountain (baptismal font)
7. Nehemiah 13:11	stations (of the cross)
8. Leviticus 7:9	oven
9. Job 19:24	pens or pencils
10. Deuteronomy 11:20	doorpost or gate

1. Divide your group into teams of two or three people and give each team a Bible, a pencil, a sheet of paper, a different verse citation from your list. Explain that when you give the signal to begin, the teams are to find their verse in the Bible. The verse will contain the name of an object that can be found in the parish or school complex. They are to go to that object to get their next verse clue.

Each team should write on its paper the name of each verse it finds (including the one you gave it to begin with) and the name of the object it refers to. The verses must be listed in the order in which they are found—no skipping around. The first team to bring you its completed list of all ten verses and object names (or whatever number is on your list) in correct order is declared the winner.

Give whatever additional directions are needed—no running, yelling, pushing, and so on—to ensure appropriate behavior. And stress that the citation slips attached to the items must *not* be removed.

2. Give the signal to begin. One leader with whom the teams can check in should remain centrally located. Other leaders should wander through the facility to give encouragement and help groups that have trouble. Wait until all the teams check in before announcing winners and awarding prizes.

Visual Bible Book Names

This activity uses a proven memory technique for helping young people (or anyone) remember the names of the books of the Bible.

Skill area. access

Age level. younger and older adolescents

Materials needed. newsprint, markers

1. Select a section of Bible books that you want the young people to memorize the names of, for example, the Pentateuch, the first seven historical books in the Old Testament, the Gospels, or the first seven letters in the New Testament. Tell the young people that you are going to enlist their help in creating a visual-cue diagram to memorize the names of these books. For each book ask them to identify something you can draw that will remind them of the name of that book. It has to be an object, not a word. It doesn't matter how the object is connected to the book name as long as the association is clear to the group. As they identify an object for each book name, draw it on the newsprint.

For example, if you were trying to memorize the names of the books of the Pentateuch, you might draw the following items.

Book name	Object to draw
Genesis	trees (symbolizing life)
Exodus	exit sign (sounds like "Exodus")
Leviticus	pair of jeans (Levi brand name)
Numbers	1, 2, 3, 4, 5 (sequence of numbers)
Deuteronomy	a dew drop and an o (Sounds like *deutero*)

2. After you have created your list, point to each object and have the young people call out together the book name associated with it. Do this several times. Do it once more at the end of your gathering. Do it once or twice more each time you gather for the next several weeks. After three or four weeks, your group will have the book names memorized in order without needing the diagram.

Silly Sentence Book Matches

Did you ever memorize something like "My very excellent mother just served us nine pies" to remember the order of the planets? You can use the same principle to help young people memorize the order of books in the Bible.

Skill area. access

Age level. younger adolescents

Materials needed. dictionaries, newsprint, markers

1. Pick a section of Bible books that you want the young people to memorize (see previous activity, "Visual Bible," for suggestions). Form small groups. Arm your group members with Bibles and dictionaries and invite them to create in their small group a memorization sentence. Each word of the sentence should sound like or begin with the same letter as one of the books you are memorizing. The words should also be in the same order as the books are in the Bible. For example, a sentence for the first nine epistles might be "Roaming corporal coroners gallantly effect philanthropic, colossal, thespian theses" (Romans, 1 Corinthians, 2 Corinthians, Galatians, Ephesians, Philippians, Colossians, 1 Thessalonians, 2 Thessalonians).

They can use the dictionaries to find words that begin with the same letters as the books. Of course the result will probably be a nonsensical sentence, but usually the more outrageous the sentence, the easier it is to memorize.

2. After each small group has created its sentence, write it on a sheet of newsprint. Say it several times as a group and then point to each word and have the young people name the Bible book it represents. Continue this during future meetings, and soon they will have the book names and their order memorized.

Bible Who's Who Timeline

This activity creates a timeline of important people in the Bible.

Skill area. big picture

Age level. younger and older adolescents

Materials needed. pens or pencils, twenty-three index cards, a 15-foot length of string, masking tape

Before the activity. Print each of the following names or set of names on a separate index card. You may also include the time period if you wish to give the young people an additional clue. Print 1900 B.C. on an index card and tape it to one end of a 15-foot-long piece of string. Print A.D. 100 on another card and tape it to the other end of the string. Create an A.D. 0 card and attach it a few feet to the left of the A.D. 100 card. Hang the string along a wall in your meeting room, with the A.D. dates on the right side.

Name	Time period
Abraham and Sarah	patriarchs and matriarchs
Jacob, Leah, and Rachel	patriarchs and matriarchs
Joseph	slavery in Egypt
Moses and Miriam	Exodus
Samson	judges
Ruth	judges
Samuel	judges
King Saul	kings and prophets
King David	kings and prophets
Solomon	kings and prophets
Elijah	kings and prophets
Isaiah	kings and prophets
Ezekiel	Exile in Babylon
Daniel	Exile in Babylon
Ezra and Nehemiah	Persian domination
Judas Maccabeus	Greek domination
Mary and Joseph	Roman domination
Jesus	Roman domination
Peter	Roman domination
Paul	Roman domination

1. Pass out the name index cards that you prepared. If your group is small, you may need to give each person two cards. If your group is larger, you may need to create more cards with additional names of biblical people. Tell everyone to use a Bible or other resource to research the person or persons on their card.

2. When everyone has finished researching their person, ask them to form a line showing the order in which these people appeared in biblical history (they are in the correct order in the list on page 34). Give them clues as necessary. For example, to help them locate Samson you might say: "After the people arrived in the Promised Land and before they had kings, they were led by people called judges. Who was a very strong judge?"

When everyone is standing in the proper order, ask them each to briefly share what they found out about their biblical character. Then attach their card to the timeline string along the wall, in the approximate proper location.

Options

- Do this activity in small groups, giving each small group a complete set of name index cards. Challenge them to be the first group to put the cards in the correct order.

- Ask the young people to find in the Bible a reference to the person or persons listed on their card, and to learn something about that person or persons, using the Bible or another resource. Give them 5 to 10 minutes to do this and assist them as needed. If they are using *The Catholic Youth Bible,* point out that many of these people can be located in the index "Events, People, and Teachings" or on the timeline. Have them present their findings to the group before putting the card on the timeline.

- Create a similar timeline that is focused on biblical events. Write on each index card the names of a different important biblical event (such as "Abraham and Sarah leave their home," "God frees the Hebrew people from Egypt," "kings rule," or "the prophets speak"). You can even do this activity twice, once with people cards and once with events cards, combining the cards on the same timeline.

Bible Journey Simulation

This is a simulation exercise in which the young people journey to different stops and act out key biblical events or periods. The idea of the simulation is briefly described here. For complete descriptions of such an activity, see session 3, "Salvation History in the Hebrew Scriptures," in *The Bible: Power and Promise* or "The First Step: A Sprint Through Salvation History," pages 14–20, in *Teaching Activities Manual for "The Catholic Youth Bible"* (both from Saint Mary's Press).

Skill area. big picture

Age level. older adolescents

Materials needed. paper; a pen; Bibles, one for each stop; a variety of props; art supplies

Before the activity. Determine the number and location of the journey stops. Possible stops include the following:
- God's covenant with Abraham and Sarah
- the Israelites' slavery in Egypt and the Exodus
- the Sinai experience
- the invasion of the Promised Land and the period of the judges
- the kings and the prophets
- the destruction of Jerusalem and the Exile in Babylon
- the return to Judah and the foreign dominations
- Jesus as the Messiah of Israel

Prepare Scripture passages and commentaries to use at the stops. Collect props that could be used at each stop. Place a Bible at each stop.

1. Divide your group into as many teams as you have stops. Give them an overview of what each stop symbolizes, or provide a handout with that information to each group. Explain that each group is to prepare a presentation for its stop—for example, a role-play, a song, a Scripture reading, a picture, or a collage—that displays that stop's significance in salvation history. You may wish to devote a whole meeting or class period to this.

2. After the groups have had time to prepare their presentation, have all the members of the group journey from one stop to the next. At each stop the assigned team makes its presentation to the whole group.

Options
- Provide music with appropriate journey themes when traveling from stop to stop.

- Invite parents or younger students to make the journey and witness the presentations.
- At the end of the journey, lead a discussion on the experience. Ask which stops were the most meaningful, which books from the Bible corresponded to each stop, how the experiences of teens parallel those of the Jewish people in the Scriptures.

Bible Songfest

Use this activity after studying a Bible book or story to review its message or meaning.

Skill area. big picture

Age level. younger and older adolescents

Materials needed. Bibles, one for each small group; paper; pencils

Divide your group into teams of three or four youth and give each team a Bible. Assign the teams a biblical passage—it could be the same passage or different passages for each team. Direct them to create a Bible song that could teach others about their assigned passage. Suggest that they use familiar tunes and just create new words to fit them. After the teams have finished, invite them to share their songs with one another.

Song Examples
The following songs were created by a high school Old Testament class:
- To the tune of the song lyrics "The neck bone's connected to the . . .":

  The Sea of Galilee is connected to the—Jordan River.
  The Jordan River's connected to the—Dead Sea.
  Parallel to this is the Mediterranean Sea and in between is Israel.

- To the tune of "Do You Know the Way to San Jose?"

  Do you know the way to the Promised Land?
  We've been in exile so long (seventy years, more or less).
  I don't remember if it's a right or left
  to Jerusalem once we hit the Mediterranean Sea.

My grandpa was born and raised in Jerusalem.
I'm going home to find a temple and a place to worship in.
We have lots of hope for Israel.
We plan to become a mighty nation once again.

The Jesus Lens

This simple demonstration points out that to interpret the Bible in context, we must start by understanding the meaning of Jesus' life, teaching, death, and Resurrection.

Skill area. context

Age level. younger and older adolescents

Materials needed. an index card, a marker, several pairs of binoculars

Before the activity. Write the words, "Jesus is the Messiah," on an index card. Make them small enough so that the sentence cannot be read from the far side of your meeting room unless you have binoculars.

1. Ask the young people to gather at one side of the room. Hang the index card on the far wall—or at the A.D. 0 location of your Bible timeline, if you have one (see the activity "Bible Who's Who"). Invite the participants to read the card. When they are not able to, pass around the binoculars and have them try to read the card again. Ask them not to reveal what they have read until everyone has had a chance to look through the binoculars. Then ask them what they saw.

2. Pose these questions to the group:
- When interpreting the Bible, how is Jesus like the lenses of the binoculars? [Because of his life, teaching, death, and Resurrection, we can more clearly see the meaning of events in the Old and New Testaments. If the card is attached to a timeline, you can make the point that you can now read clearly the events on the timeline through the lens (represented by the binoculars) of Jesus.]
- What does it mean to say that Jesus is the Messiah? [Jesus is the Promised One, the one the Jewish people were waiting for to set them free again.]

How the Bible Came to Be

Use this simulation to help the young people understand the stages in the development of the Bible. For an expanded description of this activity, see pages 40–43 of *The Bible: Power and Promise*.

Skill area. context

Age level. older adolescents

Materials needed. paper, pencils

1. Stage a dramatic event at the beginning of your class or meeting. Perhaps your pastor can come in looking desperately for the church keys. Make sure the event involves some emotion, prayer, and even humor.

2. Announce to the group that this event gives you an idea for demonstrating how the Bible was developed. Begin by creating teams of two or three people and asking the teams to discuss for a few minutes the following questions:
- What was the person involved feeling during the incident?
- How did the group get involved?
- What role did God or the person's faith play?
- What moral lesson or conclusion can they draw from what happened?

3. After the discussions assign each team the task of writing a short account of what just occurred, but each team must take a different perspective from among these choices:
- a straight news report
- a humorous story
- a story that emphasizes the group's role
- a story that illustrates the spiritual dimension
- a poem that emphasizes the lesson to be learned
- a proverb or a story with a moral

Give everyone 5 to 10 minutes to create their written account. When they are finished, ask each team to read what it has created.

4. Now create new teams by combining two teams. Direct these new teams to create a new story, combining elements from their original stories. When they are done, have each group read its new, combined story to the entire group.

5. Finish with a brief presentation making the following points about the parallels between this process and the stages in the development of the Bible.

- *Stage 1: Events and experiences.* The Bible grew out of real experiences in the lives of the Jewish people and the early Christians, just as the group had an experience that eventually prompted their writing.
- *Stage 2: Oral tradition.* Before many of the Bible's stories were written down, they were told from group to group, from generation to generation, as oral stories. This parallels the group's initial discussion about the meaning of its experience.
- *Stage 3: Written and edited tradition.* Over time, as writing became more commonplace, the important oral traditions were written down. Often these written traditions had a specific purpose or perspective, just as the teams' first written account did. Many of the original written traditions were revised and combined with other writings just as those of the class were.
- *Stage 4: The formation of the canon.* One more step was involved in the creation of the Bible we have today. Out of all the different writings from the Jewish people and the early Christians, the church had to decide which books best revealed God's saving action. The final selection of books is called the canon. In the class activity, a parallel action would be if the group had gone one more step and decided which of the final stories best revealed the real meaning of its initial experience.

Brian Singer-Towns is on the editorial staff of Saint Mary's Press and is the general editor of *The Catholic Youth Bible.* He wrote two Scripture courses in the Horizons Program, *The Bible: Power and Promise* and *Paul: The Man and the Message.* Brian has many years of experience in using the Scriptures with youth in religious education and youth ministry.

Bible Activities for Junior High Youth

Maryann Hakowski

In this chapter Maryann Hakowski shares some of her favorite Bible-based youth activities. These can be used in classrooms, meetings, and retreats. These activities are intended for junior high youth, but many of them can be adapted for use with high school youth.

The following Scripture activities are some of my favorites because they engage young people in active learning. Most of us learn more by experiencing and doing rather than sitting and listening. Imagination and creativity help move the Scriptures off the written page and help young people make the connection to experiences and situations in their own life.

These activities can be used as part of a youth group meeting, a religious education class, a retreat exercise, or a homily. For example, "Parable Characters" is great for the start of a retreat or meeting. "Jesus Suffers with Those Who Suffer" is appropriate for Good Friday, but would also be fitting for a night prayer after a day retreat reflecting on the person of Jesus.

Biblical Bookmarks

This activity can be used to create bookmarks for the group's personal use or to make gifts for other groups, such as shut-ins or younger children.

Type of activity. a craft, a service project

Related Scripture passage. any Bible passage

Materials needed. poster board or construction paper cut into approximately 2½-by-8-inch strips, pens, markers, magazines, used Christmas cards or other types of religious cards, glue

Before the activity. Consider preprinting the back of the blank bookmarks with your parish name, Mass times, contact information, and so on.

1. Instruct the group members to search for Bible verses that would work well on a bookmark. You may wish to have them limit their search to a particular book, such as the Psalms, Proverbs, a Gospel, or Ephesians. If you have enough time, let the group members share their possible verse ideas with one another. To save time you could select a Scripture passage ahead of time and assign everyone to create a bookmark using that passage. For example, you might use Ps. 23:1–2 on bookmarks for shut-ins.

2. Once they have chosen their verses, or you have assigned a passage, direct the young people to carefully write or print their chosen verses on the bottom two-thirds of a blank bookmark. Then direct them to decorate the top third of the bookmark with a drawing or a picture cut from a magazine or a used Christmas card or some other type of religious card. Suggest that if they have time, they may want to decorate the back of the bookmark too.

Consider having the completed bookmarks laminated before you distribute them.

Peace Quilt

Type of activity. a craft, a justice project

Related Scripture passages. Isa. 58:6–14; Matt. 5:9,38–48; John 14:27

Materials needed. 1-foot-square pieces of felt or fabric, one for each participant; permanent markers; a variety of fabric scraps; scissors; fabric glue; a sewing machine

1. Give each of the young people a 1-foot-square piece of felt or fabric. Set out markers, fabric scraps, and glue, and direct the young people to use these items to create a message of peace on their quilt square using words and symbols. Suggest that they make up their own quotes or use quotes about peace from the Bible. Tell them that they may focus on peace in the family, peace in the neighborhood, or peace in the world.

2. When the teens have finished working, give them an opportunity to share the meaning of their quilt squares with the group. If you have additional time, lead a discussion on the following questions:
- What are the causes of violence and hatred in our society?
- What can we do to follow Jesus' command to become peacemakers?

3. Stitch the squares together into one large quilt. Hang this quilt in your meeting space, school lobby, or parish commons as a message and reminder of the need to work for peace in our families, community, and world.

Witness Wear

Type of activity. a craft

Related Scripture passage. Matt. 22:15–21

Materials needed. poster board, one 9½-by-12-inch sheet for each person; markers; a clothesline; clothespins

Before the activity. For each participant draw an outline of a T-shirt (see page 44 for an example) on each side of a 9½-by-12-inch piece of poster board. Use the whole space.

1. Read aloud Matt. 22:15–21.

2. Invite the young people to give to God what is God's by asking them to design T-shirts that share the faith. You may want to introduce this activity in the following way:

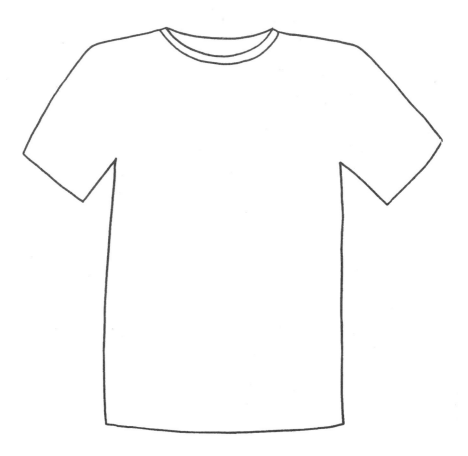

- One of the ways we show our support of music groups and sports teams is by wearing clothes and jewelry and other items with logos or photos. T-shirts are a popular way to let others know what we like, what we support, and even what we believe in.

3. Distribute markers and give each teen one of the poster board T-shirts that you prepared before the session. Direct everyone to design a shirt that proclaims their faith—that tells others what they believe in and how important God is in their life. Encourage them to be creative—to use words and symbols, to use wit and catchy slogans.

4. Invite the young people to gather into small groups to share what they put on their shirt, and why. Display their work on a clothesline so others in your parish or school can read the front and back of the witness T-shirts.

Treasure in the Scriptures

This treasure hunt encourages the young people to work together to find treasure in today's Scripture passages. The activity shows the Word of God as treasure, but also shows young people that they are a treasure to one another.

Type of activity. a game that teaches

Related Scripture passages. 1 Kings 3:5,7–12; Psalm 119; Matt. 13:44–52; Rom. 8:28–30

Materials needed. Bibles, one for each person; copies of the treasure hunt clues below, one for each small group

1. Divide the young people into teams and give each team a Bible and a copy of the treasure hunt clues below. Explain the treasure hunt process as follows:

- Look up and read aloud the first Scripture passage below. Then hunt for the items listed for that passage. After you've found as many of the items as you can, read the next passage and find the items related to that passage. Continue in this fashion until you have read each passage and found its related items.

If you like, offer bonus points to any group of young people who can find additional items and connect them with one of the Scripture passages.

Reading 1. 1 Kings 3:5,7–12. Search for . . .
something with heart
something that can be counted
something right
something wrong
something that shows understanding

Reading 2. Psalm 119. Search for . . .
something with words
something both silver and gold
something that sheds light
something with rules on it
something comforting

Reading 3. Matt. 13:44–52. Search for . . .
something that holds a treasure
something with a bead or a pearl
something that is a container
something that is old
something that is new

Reading 4. Rom. 8:28–30. Search for . . .
something that works together
something with an image of Jesus
something that gives glory to God

2. When you think that everyone has had enough time to hunt, gather them together and ask a spokesperson from each team to tell the others what his or her team found. If any team uses a person for one or more of the items, compliment the team members on their creativity.

3. When finished, mention that many of these things can describe people as well as objects. The treasures described in the Bible are made real when people live in response to God's call. Encourage the young people to keep looking for hidden treasure in the Scriptures and in one another.

Open Your Eyes, Open Your Ears

Type of activity. a game, a reflection

Related Scripture passage. Mark 7:31–37

Materials needed. earplugs, a set for each person (or two cotton balls for each person); Bibles, one for each person; blindfolds, one for each person

1. Give each participant a set of earplugs. Direct everyone to put the earplugs in their ears so they are unable to hear anything. (An alternative would be for you to stand on the other side of a large window where the participants can see you but not hear you.)

2. When no one is able to hear you, read aloud the Gospel reading for the coming Sunday. When you are finished, ask the young people to take out their earplugs and tell you what the Gospel was about. Ask:

- What are some things that make us deaf to the Word of God?
- Are there times when you can hear the Gospel proclaimed, but you still aren't really listening?

3. Give each teen a Bible and a blindfold. Ask the young people to put on their blindfold and make sure they are not able to see at all. Direct them not to remove the blindfold until told to do so. Next ask them to turn to the specific page where this Gospel is found and allow time for them to read it. Ask:
- What are some of the things that make us blind to the Word of God?
- Are there times when you have been instructed to read from the Bible, but you still weren't really understanding?

4. Allow the young people to take off their blindfold. Talk about how we need to spend time with God, to pay attention in order to see God's Word around us. Stress the need for quiet—to hear less and speak less— to make room for God. In silence we can see God better, listen to God better, and speak to God more clearly.

5. Give the young people plenty of room to spread out and create their own quiet space. Insist on quiet during this time. Ask the young people to spend 10 minutes reading Mark 7:31–37 and answering the following questions:
- How can we move from spiritual deafness to really listening to the Word of God?
- How can we move from spiritual blindness to seeing the Word of God all around us?

Parable Characters

Type of activity. an icebreaker game, a community builder

Related Scripture passages. Matt. 13:1–9, the parable of the sower and the seed; Matt. 13:44–46, the parable of the pearl and hidden treasure; Mark 4:21–23, the parable of the lamp under the bushel basket; Luke 10:25–37, the parable of the good Samaritan; Luke 12:13–21, the parable of the rich fool; Luke 13:6–9, the parable of the barren fig tree; Luke 15:1–7, the parable of the lost sheep; Luke 15:11–32, the parable of the prodigal son; Luke 18:9–14, the parable of the Pharisee and the tax collector

Materials needed. white 3-by-5-inch index cards, a marker, masking tape

Before the activity. Write on each of several 3-by-5-inch index cards the name of a different parable character or item, for example: a shepherd, a lost sheep, a pearl, a fig tree, a lamp under a bushel basket, a lamp shining, a rich fool, a Pharisee, a tax collector, a sower, a seed, a seed among thorns, a good seed, a seed on dry land, the prodigal son, the prodigal son's father, the prodigal son's brother, the good Samaritan, the robber, the Levite. Make a card for each person in your group.

1. Tape on the back of each person in your group one of the cards that you prepared. Each person should be unable to see the name of the character on his or her own back.

2. Instruct the participants to try to guess their character by how people respond to them. If needed, share the following examples:
- If you are a seed from the parable of the sower and the seed, someone may encourage you to grow.
- If you are the lost sheep, someone may pretend to find you.

Leave the Devil in the Desert

This activity takes the simple childhood game commonly called Monkey in the Middle and turns it into an illustration of how to follow Jesus' example when we meet the devil—in the desert of our life.

Related Scripture passage. Luke 4:1–13

Type of activity. a game that teaches

Materials needed. a ball

1. Ask the young people to stand in a circle, facing in. Explain that the circle represents the Christian community. Ask for a volunteer to be the first "devil" and instruct her or him to stand in the middle of the circle. Also explain that the ball used in this game represents faith.

2. When everyone is in position, give the following directions:
- The object of the game is to pass the ball (faith) from one person to another without the devil taking it away. In other words, we are trying to

"keep the faith." The devil is trying to do whatever she or he can to steal faith as it is tossed from person to person. If the devil temporarily steals faith away, the last person with the ball becomes the new devil for the next round of the game.

3. After playing the game for a while, relate it to the Gospel reading, Luke 4:1–13:

- What can we do to avoid temptation?
- What did Jesus do to show us how we should treat the devil?
- How can we ask God's help in times of temptation?

Jesus Suffers with Those Who Suffer

This prayer was originally designed for Good Friday, but it may also be shared after praying the stations of the cross.

Type of activity. a prayer, a reflection

Related Scripture passages. Luke 22:39–42,47–48,54–57; Luke 23:44–46; John 19:1–3,14–15,16–18

Materials needed. newspaper clippings (collect six examples of suffering from local and national newspapers); a copy or copies of the prayer script below, one for each reader

Before the activity. The week before you use this prayer, clip from newspapers six stories that involve suffering. Use local and national newspapers so that you can collect clips about local, state, national, and international events. It is best to also include examples of suffering both endured by teens and caused by teens.

Number the clippings from 1 to 6 and highlight just a few of the most relevant sentences of each one.

1. Ask for a volunteer to read the Scripture passages in the following script (reader 1). And ask for another volunteer to read the highlighted sections of each newspaper clipping (reader 2). Give them each a copy of the following script, and give the newspaper reader the clippings. Let them have a few moments to prepare. (Or, if your group is large, you could involve more people by asking a different person to read each part of the prayer script.)

2. Gather the group in the prayer area and ask the first reader to begin:

Reader 1. Jesus left the city and went to the Mount of Olives, and the disciples went with him. When he arrived at the place, he said to them, "Pray that you will not fall into temptation." Then he went off from them about a distance of a stone's throw and knelt down and prayed. "Father, if you will, take this cup of suffering away from me. Not my will, however, but your will be done." [Based on Luke 22:39–42, GNB]

Reader 2. [Read aloud the highlighted portion of newspaper clipping 1.]

Reader 1. A crowd arrived, led by Judas, one of the twelve disciples. He came up to Jesus to kiss him. But Jesus said, "Judas, is it with a kiss that you betray the Son of Man?" [Based on Luke 22:47–48, GNB]

Reader 2. [Read aloud the highlighted portion of newspaper clipping 2.]

Reader 1. They arrested Jesus and took him to the house of the high priest; Peter followed at a distance. A fire had been lit in the center of the courtyard, and Peter joined those who were sitting around it. When one of the servant girls saw him, she looked straight at him and said, "This man was with Jesus!" But Peter denied it, "Woman, I don't even know him!" [Based on Luke 22:54–57, GNB]

Reader 2. [Read aloud the highlighted portion of newspaper clipping 3.]

Reader 1. Pilate took Jesus and had him whipped. The soldiers made a crown of thorny branches and put it on his head; then they put a purple robe on him and said, "Long live the king of the Jews!" And they went up and slapped him. [Based on John 19:1–3, GNB]

Reader 2. [Read aloud the highlighted portion of newspaper clipping 4.]

Reader 1. It was almost noon of the day before Passover. Pilate said to the people, "Here is your king!" They shouted back, "Kill him! Kill him! Crucify him! Crucify him!" [Based on John 19:14–15, GNB]

Reader 2. [Read aloud the highlighted portion of newspaper clipping 5.]

Reader 1. Pilate handed Jesus over to be crucified. The soldiers took Jesus out, and he carried his cross to Golgotha, which means "the place of the skull." There they crucified him. [Based on John 19:16–18, GNB]

Reader 2. [Read aloud the highlighted portion of newspaper clipping 6.]

Reader 1. It was twelve o'clock when the sun stopped shining and darkness covered the whole country and the curtain in the Temple was torn in two. Jesus cried out in a loud voice: "Father! In your hands I place my spirit!" Then he bowed his head and died. [Based on Luke 23:44–46, GNB]

Prayer of Love

Type of activity. a prayer, an affirmation

Related Scripture passage. Eph. 1:3–14

Before the activity. Insert the names of all your group members into the Prayer of Love found below. Make sure everyone's name is included. If you have more than ten group members, put two or three names in each blank, as needed, and adjust the wording for sense.

1. Share the following prayer as part of an evening prayer service, as a blessing at the end of a session, or as a prayer before a written or verbal individual affirmation activity.

- *Prayer of Love*
  Grace and peace to _____ from God, our creator, and the Lord Jesus Christ.
      Praised be the God of our Lord Jesus Christ, who has bestowed on _____ in Christ every spiritual blessing in the heavens! God chose _____ before the world began to be holy and blameless in God's sight, to be full of love; God likewise predestined _____ through Jesus Christ to be God's adopted sons and daughters. Such was the Creator's will and pleasure that _____ might praise the glorious favor God has bestowed on them in the Beloved.
      It is in Christ and through his blood that _____ has been redeemed and her [or his] sins forgiven, so immeasurably generous is God's favor to you. God has given _____ the wisdom to understand fully the mystery of the plan the Creator was pleased to decree in Christ, to be carried out in the fullness of time, namely, to bring all things in the heavens and on earth under Christ.
      In Christ _____ was chosen, and in the decree of God, who administers everything according to God's will and counsel, _____ was predestined to praise God's glory by being the first to hope in Christ. In him _____ was chosen—when you first heard the glad tidings of salvation, the word of truth, and believed in it.

The Voice of Thomas

Type of activity. prayer, journaling

Related Scripture passage. John 20:19–31

Materials needed. a Bible; pens or pencils; journals, one for each person

1. Dim the lights in the room and ask the young people to quietly make themselves comfortable. Invite someone to read aloud John 20:19–31.

2. Ask the young people to close their eyes and listen to the voice of Thomas and imagine what Thomas might have been thinking before and after Jesus appeared to him. Then read aloud the following script:

- *The voice of Thomas*
  I thought they were crazy—a bunch of men gone mad by grief, mad enough to believe in ghosts. The doors were locked; no one could get into that room.

  I told them to prove it to me, prove to me that they had seen Jesus walk again on the earth. When I see the places the nails cut his flesh— then I will believe.

  How I was to regret those words. Soon he stood before me—my Lord and my God—in the flesh, offering to let me examine his hands, put my hand in his side.

  I deserved to be cast out for my doubt. How could I have doubted my friend, my savior, my Lord?

  Yet he did not send me away. He said, "Peace be with you." And never have I felt such peace.

  My Lord and my God!

3. Ask the young people to spend some time writing in their journal about times when they have had doubts about their faith, and a prayer asking God's help in overcoming those doubts, or thanking God for the help they received in overcoming those doubts.

We Are the Body of Christ

Type of activity. prayer

Related Scripture passage. 1 Cor. 12:12–27

Materials needed. yarn, a Bible, transparent tape

Before the activity. Ask a volunteer to lie down in the center of your meeting space. Use yarn to make an outline of the person's body. Use dark yarn on a light floor and light yarn on a dark floor. Use transparent tape to secure the yarn outline in place.

1. Gather the young people in a circle around the yarn figure and read aloud 1 Cor. 12:12–27.

2. Invite the young people—one at a time—to complete the phrase, "I can build up the Body of Christ by _____."

3. They should stand next to the part of the body their prayer reflects. For example, someone might stand by the ear and say, "I can build up the Body of Christ by listening to others when they are down." Explain that after they have taken their place on the yarn body, they should remain standing there until everyone has become part of the Body of Christ.

Maryann Hakowski has been a youth minister since 1982, serving as a retreat director, diocesan youth minister, and parish pastoral associate in Pennsylvania, Virginia, and Illinois. She is the author of several widely used publications on retreats, prayer, and youth group activities, including two series from Saint Mary's Press, Sharing the Sunday Scriptures with Youth and Vine and Branches.

Bible Activities
for Senior High Youth

Tony Tamberino

In his chapter Tony Tamberino shares some of the creative ways he has developed for making the Bible come alive for senior high youth. Most of his activities are designed for senior high youth, but many of them can be adapted for junior high teens. Tony's energy and enthusiasm are contagious, and many of his ideas will become part of your youth and Scripture repertoire.

Several years ago I was stunned, and feeling a bit defensive, as I read the evaluations from a high school retreat I had just finished. Under suggestions for improvement, I read, "Please drop all that stuff about the Bible" and "Forget that Bible study—it's boring and who can understand it anyway?" Almost a third of the sixty-five participants expressed similar feelings! I really believed that what I had presented was interesting and relevant to the lives of young people, but a significant number of that sophomore class found the presentations and activities using the Bible boring, irrelevant, and a waste of their time.

My response? I have gone back to the drawing board and sought advice from the young people themselves. I borrowed some ideas from others. I developed some original approaches of my own. And guess what? I found that through these creative approaches, the Bible's stories started to become real and meaningful for the teens I was working with. The negative attitudes toward the Bible started to disappear. The following strategies and activities are part of this new repertoire. I hope that the activities will also help your teens become enthusiastic toward the Scriptures.

Strategies

Continuing the Dialogue

"Continuing the dialogue" is one technique that helps young people enter into Bible stories. Through a couple of different approaches, I ask them to imagine that they are characters in a particular story. How would they respond to the situation? Although this approach is certainly not original, it often strikes teens as a novel way to think about Scripture stories. Senior high teens can pose some interesting questions and responses as they imagine and continue the biblical stories.

Using Children's Literature

One of the ways I love to pray with young people and adults is with children's literature, especially books with beautiful artwork. Many of these books have either direct or indirect references to the Bible. My methodology is very simple: (1) I start by reading the children's book to the group; (2) I ask for volunteers to share what message they heard and how it made them feel; (3) I read a Scripture passage that echoes or elaborates on the book's theme; and (4) I ask for volunteers to share how the Scripture passage and the message of the children's book are related. Occasionally I'll use prepared discussion questions or an activity to help make the connection.

Here are a few examples of books and some ideas on how they might be applied to Bible lessons and passages.

Old Turtle

Old Turtle, by Douglas Wood (Duluth, MN: Pfeifer-Hamilton Publishers, 1992), provides a wonderful opportunity to talk about the beauties of creation, the value and dignity of all life, care for the environment, sin, responsibility, and the "blame game." I use this book to study the Creation stories in the first three chapters of Genesis and to emphasize God's gift of dominion to humans and human responsibility for God's creation.

The Christmas Candle

The Christmas Candle, by Richard Paul Evans (New York: Simon and Schuster Books for Young Readers, 1998), was written for Christmas but delivers an appropriate and powerful message for any time of the year. I use this story when examining social-justice themes. The biblical passage I most refer to with this book is Matt. 25:31–46 (the judgment of the nations), although passages from the prophets, for example, Amos, chapter 2, and Mic. 6:6–16, can generate spirited discussion. Another Gospel passage to use in conjunction with this story is Luke 16:19–31 (the rich man and Lazarus).

The Tale of Three Trees

I frequently use *The Tale of Three Trees,* by Angela Elwell Hunt (Elgin, IL: Lion Publishing, 1989), when I speak of Jesus' death and Resurrection and how difficult it must have been for him to see his dreams for Israel and his own ministry crumble. It also provides a powerful introduction for speaking of success and failure and how both will be part of any human life. A good exercise for a teen retreat is to read aloud the story, and then direct the young people to write about a success and a failure in their life. Allow them to share their work in small groups. Such sharing can lead to honest discussion and mutual support as the young people hear stories from their peers about overcoming adversity and dealing with tough times.

Many other children's books could be used in your ministry, including the following:

Bunting, Eve. *Smoky Night.* San Diego: Harcourt Brace and Company, 1994.

Fox, Mem. *Wilfrid Gordon McDonald Partridge.* Brooklyn: Kane/Miller Book Publishers, 1985.

van Allsburg, Chris. *The Polar Express.* Boston: Houghton Mifflin Company, 1985.

Yolen, Jane. *Owl Moon.* New York: Philomel Books, 1987.

Bible-Themed Games for Groups

Games of all kinds are a perennial favorite in youth ministry. They help break the ice, build community, and raise the energy level of a group. Many old favorites such as Pictionary, charades, and twenty questions can be used with biblical stories and characters as the answers. As your knowledge of the Bible grows, you will find it easier to make these adaptations. To get you started, I offer some suggestions for Bible searches and biblical scavenger hunts later on in this chapter.

Interactive Bible Productions

Interactive Bible productions invite those with drama and performance skills to step forward and take the lead. And because most of us have a budding actor inside of us, interactive Bible productions appeal to a wide range of young people. They call on the young people's ability to act and use their imaginations to put themselves in biblical people's situations. The activities I suggest require different levels of preparation and familiarity with the biblical material—start with those that you are most comfortable with.

Activities

Completing the Story

Strategy. This activity is related to the strategy "Continuing the Dialogue."

Read a Scripture story to the teens. Then ask them to complete the story by role-playing a conversation between some of the characters in the moments following the part of the story that you read. Get everyone involved. If your group is larger than the number of characters in the story, form small groups and make sure everyone takes on a role. Give the small groups time to develop and practice their conversations. You may need to give them suggestions about how the conversation might continue. Some of my favorite stories and ideas for conversations follow.

The Rich Man (Matt. 19:16–22)

The conversation continues as the man leaves Jesus and meets a group of his friends at the edge of the crowd. The friends ask questions like, "Did you meet the Teacher?" "What did he say to you?" and "Well, what are you going to do?"

The Command to Sacrifice Isaac (Gen. 22:1–19)

The conversation continues as Isaac and Abraham discuss what just happened. Isaac talks about how he is feeling. Abraham shares how frightened he had been. Isaac and Abraham arrive back home, where Isaac talks to his mother. (Incidentally, I had one young person upon arriving home say to Sarah: "Mom, call social services. Dad just tried to kill me!")

Joseph and Mary (Matt. 1:18–19)

The conversation continues as Mary informs Joseph that she is pregnant and tries to explain the circumstances, but before Joseph has been visited by the angel in the dream.

The possibilities with this activity are infinite. You could use Nicodemus and Joseph of Arimathea (John 19:38–42), David and Bathsheba (2 Sam. 11:1–13), Jesus and Mary Magdalene after the Resurrection (John 20:11–18), Jesus and Peter at the Sea of Tiberias (John 21:15–19), Jacob and Joseph at their reunion (Gen. 46:28–34).

When everyone is ready, invite some volunteers to share their conversation with the entire group.

Taking a Part

Strategy. This activity is related to the strategy "Continuing the Dialogue."

Select a Bible passage with more than one character in it. Decide whether you want the young people to act out the passage, or simply to imagine being a character in the story as you read it aloud. When they are finished acting out the passage or you are finished reading it, ask the characters to relate what they saw, how they were affected by what happened, and what they think might result from the event.

Taking a part is particularly effective for shared homilies at Masses or at prayer experiences with young people. Stories from the Gospels seem to work the best. It is important that whoever facilitates this shared reflection asks questions that are open ended and allow for creative imagining. Again, some of my favorite stories for this approach follow.

The Man with a Withered Hand (Mark 3:1–6)

Some people take the part of Jesus, the healed man, the Pharisees, or the Herodians. Others may take the parts of random members of the crowd.

The Wedding at Cana (John 2:1–12)

People take the parts of Jesus and Mary, the attendants, the chief steward, the wedding couple, and Jesus' disciples.

Other effective Bible passages for use with this approach include Jesus feeding the multitude (Matt. 15:32–39), the Gadarene demoniacs (Matt. 8:28–34), and the story of Zacchaeus (Luke 19:1–10).

 Bible Searches

Strategy. This activity is related to the strategy "Bible-Themed Games for Groups."

Some of the easiest activities to arrange are Bible-search games, in which young people work in groups to find particular passages, characters, or lists. Group your young people in pairs or small groups, distribute a list of items that they need to find in their Bibles (see the list below), and let them begin. The outcome? Young people paging through the Bible looking for information and having fun. Learning by osmosis! It is always a good idea to have candy bars ready for whoever finishes the list first. The following list offers a few of the possibilities for Bible searches. The answers are provided in brackets.

- the books of the Pentateuch [Genesis, Exodus, Leviticus, Numbers, Deuteronomy]
- the names of the original Twelve Apostles [Simon Peter, James (son of Zebedee), John, Andrew, Philip, Bartholomew, Matthew, Thomas, James (son of Alphaeus), Thaddaeus, Simon, Judas (Mark 3:16–19)]
- the seven signs (miracles) in the Gospel of John [wedding feast at Cana (2:1–12), cure of the royal official's son (4:46–54), cure at the pool of Bethsaida (5:2–9), miracle of the loaves (6:1–14), walking on water (6:16–21), cure of the man born blind (9:1–12), and the raising of Lazarus (11:38–44)]
- the plagues visited on Egypt [water turned to blood, frogs, gnats, flies, diseased livestock, boils, thunder and hail, locusts, darkness, death of the firstborn (Exodus, chapters 7–12)]
- the Ten Commandments [see Exod. 20:1–17]
- the Bible passage where Saul gets knocked off his horse [there is no horse—a chance to teach about Bible misconceptions; see Acts 9:1–31]
- the story of the Magi (wise men) [this is only found in Matt. 2:1–12— a chance to point out that each Gospel has a different version of Jesus' birth]

- the spiritual gifts [wisdom, knowledge, faith, healing, the working of miracles, prophecy, discernment, various kinds of tongues, the interpretation of tongues (1 Cor. 12:4–10)]
- all four Gospel stories about the cleansing of the Temple [Matt. 21:12–17; Mark 11:15–19; Luke 19:45–48; John 2:13–25]

The passages about the cleansing of the Temple provide a great opportunity to either introduce or reinforce the Catholic approach to the Bible. A Bible search for the cleansing of the Temple (which occurs toward the end of Jesus' ministry in the synoptic Gospels of Matthew, Mark, and Luke but at the beginning of Jesus' ministry in John's Gospel) is a good way to point out the differences between the synoptic Gospels and John's Gospel. This story, and others like it, will raise questions and stimulate discussion about why such differences exist (see the chapter by Margaret Nutting Ralph). Discussions like this can go a long way in preventing an increase of Catholic fundamentalism and help develop in your young people a healthy and critical approach to Bible Study.

Biblical Scavenger Hunts

Strategy. This activity is related to the strategy "Bible-Themed Games for Groups."

Scavenger hunts are still a big hit with kids today. Although these activities require a bit more energy and preparation, they are usually well worth the effort. To create a Bible scavenger hunt, select a theme, event, or person from the Bible, and write a series of six to eight clues that would lead someone to a part of the Bible that discusses that theme, event, or person (see the examples below). Form teams of four or five people each and give each team the first clue. As each team figures out a clue, it earns the right to receive the next one. As with Bible searches, prizes and candy turn the learning into major fun. Here are a couple of my favorite Bible scavenger hunts:

- *Jesus and his miracles*
  Clue 1. Many consider it Jesus' first miracle. Search the fourth Gospel.
  Clue 2. Well you have been to Cana. Now find three miracles Jesus did in Capernaum early in his ministry. They are all in the same chapter.

Clue 3. Jesus faced opposition because he healed on the Sabbath. Find the cure of the man with the withered hand in Matthew. What were the disciples doing just before this that also angered the Pharisees?

Clue 4. A widow's son is raised from the dead—search Luke's Gospel. What is the name of her town?

Clue 5. We've all heard of the miracle of the loaves. But two Gospels actually have two miracles of the loaves. Which two Gospels are they?

Clue 6. Jesus raised one of his good friends from the dead. Name him and his two sisters. In what chapter of John is this account found?

Clue 7. At Jesus' arrest one disciple used a sword to cut off the ear of the high priest's servant. But only one Gospel has Jesus heal the man's ear. Which one?

Clue 8. In one of Jesus' healings of a possessed man, a herd of animals is destroyed. In what country does the miracle take place? What kind of animal is destroyed?

- *Prophetic visions*

  Clue 1. Find a battlefield of bones in Ezekiel. What brings the bones to life?

  Clue 2. The prophet Jeremiah saw two things immediately after his call from God. What were the two things? What did the second thing symbolize?

  Clue 3. The whole Book of Nahum is called a vision. What is the first thing the prophet describes? What happens to the seas and rivers at God's rebuke?

  Clue 4. Zechariah's prophecy contains eight visions. Find the eighth vision of the chariots. What colors were the horses of each chariot?

  Clue 5. Most of the Book of Isaiah is also considered to be a vision. Search chapter 11. Who do Christians understand the passage to be about?

  Clue 6. Some prophetic visions are included in the New Testament. In which book do they occur? On what day does the first vision take place?

  Clue 7. Find the vision of the four beasts in Daniel. Which animals do the first three beasts resemble? Who conquers the fourth beast in the end?

- *Church hymns and the Scriptures*

  Create your own clues for this topic, using your parish hymnal as your resource. For example, "This hymn is based on God's call to Samuel in 1 Samuel, chapter 3." Answer: "Here I Am, Lord." For additional fun, require that each team sing the hymns.

Bible Talk Shows

Strategy. This activity is related to the strategy "Interactive Bible Productions."

Looking to get a number of your young people up, having fun, and learning about the Bible? Produce a Bible talk show with famous Bible characters as the celebrity guests. Direct the kids to create the format and name the program. Will it be like *Oprah* or *The Tonight Show* or *Rikki Lake?* Assign people to be the interviewer, the guests, the studio audience, and the director. Ask a team of your more creative kids to develop commercials that would be appropriate for biblical times. If the talent exists, have the director "hire" a couple of musicians. Also tell the director to be sure to include time for questions from the audience. Help the director select the guest list (see the possibilities and their Bible citations below), then distribute the citations and encourage the actors to look up their passage in order to prepare their character's responses.

You might want to spread this activity over two sessions, one for preparation and one for performance.

- Moses and Pharaoh (Exod. 5:1–23)
- Samson and Delilah (Judges, chapter 16)
- Ruth, Naomi, and Boaz (entire Book of Ruth)
- David and Jonathan (1 Samuel, chapter 20)
- Elijah, Ahab, and Jezebel (1 Kings, chapter 21)
- John the Baptist and Herod (Mark 6:14–29)
- Mary and Joseph (Matt. 1:18–25)
- Peter, James, and John (Luke 9:28–39)
- Judas and Peter (John 18:1–27)
- Jairus, his wife, and his daughter (Luke 8:40–56)
- Paul and Barnabas (Acts 11:19–26 and 15:36–41)

The Jesus Chair

Strategy. This activity is related to the strategy "Interactive Bible Productions."

A common catechetical activity is to ask young people to write down a "serious" question that they would ask Jesus if he were living among us as he did two thousand years ago. You can go one step beyond that by having the young people not only write the questions but also take turns answering them as they think Jesus would. Seek volunteers to be Jesus and invite them to sit in the "Jesus chair."

You, as the adult leader, should be ready to clarify and elaborate on the answers given by the various Jesuses. The end result, though, is often spirited and honest discussion around faith topics, Catholic values, and church teaching. The added dimension of having the teens struggle to get into the mind of Christ proves to be an invaluable experience. I usually conclude this activity with a group reading of Phil. 2:5–11. Arrange the canticle in Psalm form reciting the verses antiphonally, but include the line, "Your attitude must be Christ's," as a refrain after each verse. The entire group should proclaim the last verse in unison, "Jesus Christ is Lord to the glory of God!

Bible Skits

Strategy. This activity is related to the strategy "Interactive Bible Productions."

Bible skits is a technique that can be used over and over again because the outcome is never the same. Brainstorm with the young people a list of Bible passages or events that would work in a skit (see some possibilities listed below). Break everyone into small groups and let each group choose one passage or event and put together a skit or role-play based on it. Urge them to be creative, to be just this side of outrageous, to go to the edge and make their skit or role-play relevant for today. One young man actually called them extreme Bible skits!

Be sure to have plenty of props available, for example, balloons, bandannas, markers, poster board, stuffed animals, and, of course, the ever present bag of candy bars. One last suggestion that I have found to be very helpful: have someone from the small group read the corresponding Bible passage either before or after the skit's presentation.

The Parables of Jesus
- the sower (Mark 4:1–9)
- the good Samaritan (Luke 10:25–37)

- the talents (Matt. 25:14–30)
- weeds among the wheat (Matt. 13:24–30,36–43)
- laborers in the vineyard (Matt. 20:1–16)

Study of the parables provides an opportunity to speak of the differences among the Gospels. Occasionally I will ask the young people to act out one of the parables from John's Gospel. Naturally, questions are raised when they can find no parables in John, and you can share some insights about why each Gospel writer chose to write as he did.

The Miracles of Jesus
- the calming of the storm (Mark 4:35–41)
- the feeding of five thousand (John 6:1–15)
- the cleansing of ten lepers (Luke 17:11–19)

Other Biblical Events
- Pentecost and the descent of the Spirit (Acts 2:1–13)
- the giving of the Ten Commandments (Exod. 19:16—20:18)
- Ananias and Sapphira (Acts 5:1–11)
- the crossing of the Red Sea (Exod. 14:1–30)

Bible Debates

Strategy. This activity is related to the strategy "Interactive Bible Productions."

Another activity that challenges young people to articulate their faith and face some of the obstacles that culture and society can present to people of faith is to debate about Biblical teaching. In particular, some of the "hard" teachings of Jesus can make for effective debates. In preparation for this activity, select one of Jesus' teachings as a debate topic and prepare position statements, one for the teaching, and one against it. Here are just a few prospects for debate topics, along with a pro and con position statement for each:

The Beatitudes (Matt. 5:1–12)
Pro. "The Beatitudes are a perfectly reasonable way for a committed follower of Jesus to live.

Con. "The Beatitudes are really a bit too much. No one can live like that today and be successful."

The Workers in the Vineyard (Matt. 20:1–16)
Pro. "The story shows that none of us can earn God's love and salvation; it's given freely to all who accept it. God's sense of fairness is much bigger than ours."

Con. "The story isn't fair. Those people who worked a longer day should receive more than those who worked less. It's a question of justice."

Love for Enemies (Luke 6:27–36)
Pro. "Only by loving our enemies can we overcome the cycle of violence in our world. Jesus challenges us to love recklessly, to reject vengeance in order to change the world."

Con. "Jesus is way over the edge on this one. This attitude is not only crazy, it is dangerous. We should never let ourselves be taken advantage of."

The Bread from Heaven (John 6:22–59)
Just a brief comment concerning this passage from John. Jesus' teaching on his giving his body and blood as real food and drink and the church's subsequent teaching on the Eucharist are important topics for today's Catholic teens. A debate such as this is an excellent way to reaffirm the Catholic understanding of the Eucharist and the teaching on the Real Presence.

Pro. "When bread and wine are consecrated at Mass it really becomes the body and blood of Jesus. Jesus is very clear about this, and he isn't speaking symbolically here."

Con. "We really need to update our language. We don't really eat the body and drink the blood of Christ. It may be blessed, but it is still bread and wine."

When you are ready to begin, divide the group into two teams (or more for larger groups). Assign one group to defend the teaching and the other to present arguments against it. Give them their respective position statements to help them focus and prepare. Invite them to begin, with only two people debating at a time. After each presentation invite questions from the audience.

Prophets Today

This activity uses the notion of prophecy and the role of the prophet both in ancient Israel and in New Testament times to encourage young people to apply biblical teaching to contemporary life. Introduce this activity by emphasizing that the biblical prophets were messengers of God's Word, not primarily fortunetellers. Then ask the young people to identify people in today's world or in recent history who might qualify as prophets. Finally, go a step further by challenging the young people to think of themselves as prophets. Ask: "What do you think God would have you say to his people at this time in history? Is there any particular group, for example, the United States, world leaders, the church, big business, pro athletes, that God would send you to?" Let the young people work alone or in groups of two or three to write their own prophecy. The results can be startling!

Biblical Collages

Although the idea of high schoolers working with glue and scissors may at first seem like a developmental miscue, I have found that they love the opportunity to collaborate and have fun with creating collages. Provide the necessary art supplies. Identify various scriptural topics that they might base a collage on—assign a few particular passages or choose one passage and have different small groups work on it separately. A few possibilities follow:

- the Eucharist and hunger
- 1 Corinthians, chapter 13
- the face of Christ
- Ecclesiastes, chapter 3
- modern-day plagues
- the cry for justice

Conclusion

As with any activity with young people, the sharing and teaching of the Scriptures may appear to be a daunting task. We must not, however, be put off or discouraged, for we are sharing our faith and our own relationship with God. In moments of frustration, remember the words of Jeremiah:

> If I say, "I will not mention [God],
>> or speak any more in his name,"
>> then within me there is something like a burning fire
>>> shut up in my bones;
>> I am weary with holding it in,
>>> and I cannot.

(20:9)

The choice to share God's Word is not entirely our own; we have been chosen!

Tony Tamberino has been active in youth ministry for thirty years. He has served as a parish director of religious education and a parish coordinator of youth ministry. He has also taught religious studies and theology at the secondary, undergraduate, and graduate levels. Tony is the associate for youth and young adult ministry at Saint John the Evangelist Parish in Columbia, Maryland.

Teaching *Lectio Divina* to Young People

Lisa-Marie Calderone-Stewart

In this chapter, Lisa-Marie Calderone-Stewart shares how a very old technique for reading the Bible is being used effectively with young people today. In fact, this treasured Catholic tradition is finding a home with many other Christian denominations. Once you experience its simplicity, you will find that opportunities abound for sharing it with young people.

Lectio divina is Latin for "divine reading." It is the name of an ancient way for praying with the Bible that comes to us out of the Benedictine tradition. When introducing this technique to your teens, their first question might be, "What's so divine about reading?" But don't let that stop you from using this simple, effective way to help youth become more familiar with the Scriptures and prayer.

Basically the process has four or five steps, depending on how you want to pray it. Each step has a Latin name. I will begin by describing the steps and then show four variations on how you can use them with groups of young people—or even with adults.

The Steps

Step 1. *Lectio*

Step 1 is *lectio* (lex-ee-oh), which means "reading." In the *lectio* step you simply read a Scripture passage. Read it out loud several times. Try to stress different words each time you read.

Let the words really sink in. Try to read with an open mind and heart. Let the passage speak to you. Listen carefully.

Step 2. *Meditatio*

Step 2 is *meditatio* (med-it-tots-ee-oh), which means "meditation." The *meditatio* step is deep thinking. Questions such as the following can help you think through the Scripture passage that you read:

- What does this passage say to me?
- Who am I in this Scripture?
- What do I see and hear?
- What do I think?
- Which character do I most relate to?
- What do I need to learn from this passage?

You might journal your answers to these questions.

Step 3. *Oratio*

Step 3 is *oratio* (or-ot-see-oh), which means "prayer." *Oratio* is deep feeling. Move into the heart of the matter. It's time to respond to God. What do you want to communicate to God? What do you most want in your relationship with God? What emotions do you want to express to God? joy? grief? fear? gratitude? Share yourself with God in your own personal way.

Step 4. *Contemplatio*

Step 4 is *contemplatio* (con-tem-plot-see-oh), which means "contemplation." *Contemplatio* is actually another form of prayer. It's the most difficult step to explain. It's the chance for us to receive God's communication to us. It's not a time for thinking; it's a time for removing all thoughts and distractions from your mind and heart. It's a time to just be passive and rest in God's love and tenderness. Don't do anything. Just be. And recognize God in that.

Step 5. *Actio*

Step 5 is *actio* (ax-ee-oh), which means "action." Actio is the optional step. It's a time to plan what you will focus on next. Do you sense a challenge from God? Is there something good that God is calling you to do? Something harmful God wants you to stop doing? What's your plan of action? Decide what to do.

Lectio divina was developed as a form of personal prayer. The original design was meant for one person, alone and in private. But the process can be easily modified and shared with a group. Here are a few ways you might introduce young people to *lectio divina*. Each of these variations works best if all the group members have their own Bible.

The Variations

Prepared Reflection Lectio Divina

This variation on *lectio divina* uses both a Bible passage and a related reflection from another source, such as an article from *The Catholic Youth Bible* (CYB) or material from a Bible commentary or Bible study program. The article or reflection questions provide discussion and reflection material to use in the *meditatio* step.

If you are using a resource like the *Catholic Youth Bible,* focus on a Bible passage accompanied by an article. I'll use Mark 4:35–41 as an example. Begin by playing some gentle music in the background. Gather the young people in a circle, and tell them that you will be exploring the *lectio divina* process. Give them the handout at the end of this chapter, "The Steps for *Lectio Divina:* Spiritual Reading," so that they can follow along with each step.

Step 1. *Lectio*

Read the selected Bible passage out loud yourself or ask a young person (a good reader) to read it. Then ask another young person (perhaps a good reader of the other gender) to read it a second time. Finally, let everyone read it one more time, silently.

Step 2. *Meditatio*

Ask someone to read the article or reflection questions that you prepared for use with the passage you just read. Then allow time to discuss the passage. If the discussion does not take off by itself, use the questions on step 2 of the *lectio divina* handout as a starting point.

For example, if you are using the Mark 4:35–41 article in the *Catholic Youth Bible,* "Life's Storms," you might start by reading the first two paragraphs of the article. Then pause and discuss the questions listed in step 2 on the *lectio divina* handout. Ask each person to share his or her answer to at least one of those questions. Let the young people pick whichever question and answer they want to share with the group.

After everyone has shared, read aloud the last paragraph of the *CYB* article. Tell the group members that they don't have to share any answers to the questions in that paragraph, but they should spend some time thinking about what their answers would be. Suggest that they might even write the answers on the back of their handout, or in a journal.

Step 3. *Oratio*

Explain that this is a time for deep feelings, a time for communicating with God. Tell them that you are going to model what that might be like. Then offer a spontaneous prayer to God, based on your feelings at this point in the *lectio divina* process.

For example, Mark 4:35–41 might prompt you to say the following prayer:

> I have to admit it, God. When there are storms, I get scared. I become afraid so easily. I start worrying if everything is going to be all right. Sometimes I start blaming other people, even when it's not really their fault at all. Help me become more brave. I want to trust you more.

If the young people in your group are accustomed to praying out loud together, invite them to share their feelings with God out loud. If they have not done this before, invite them to share at least one word or phrase that might express to God their feelings at this time.

Step 4. *Contemplatio*

Tell the group how *contemplatio*, a type of prayer, can be difficult at first. *Contemplatio* is a time to just rest in God's presence: to be passive and enjoy who God is in our lives, to settle into the tenderness of God's love, to not think, not worry, not imagine, not do anything, to just be.

Have everyone close their eyes and sit with God for a minute, longer if you think they can handle it.

Step 5. *Actio*

If you decide to use this step, explain to the group that *actio* is a time to make a resolution or to plan a course of action. This resolution or plan can be large or small, depending on the needs of each person. Give the group an example, based on your own prayer from step 3. Perhaps you have put off a big project because you were afraid of failing. Perhaps you have worried about how to tell someone something important. You decide to go now and do the thing that needs to be done.

Give the group members a few minutes to think about what they might want to do, based on their experience with this *lectio divina* process. Then ask the young people to share, even in a general way, what kind of thing they have decided to do. Tell them they are free to give some minor details but not to name any names. Explain that they can choose to be vague, simply stating that there is something they decided not to do (or to do), or that they are now ready to tell someone something.

This variation is a great teaching opportunity for the personal use of *lectio divina*. If you use this variation in a retreat setting, you may wish to follow this group experience with time for the young people to try *lectio divina* privately. Invite them to find a quiet place and go through the process on their own. Assure them that they may use any Scripture passage that interests them. If they are using the *Catholic Youth Bible,* they can use the article index to find a topic that interests them. Then let everyone spread out for the prayer time. Regather them afterward and ask them to share what the experience was like.

Lectionary-Based Lectio Divina

Lectio divina can be used with your youth to reflect on the Sunday readings. If Sunday's Gospel or first reading has an accompanying article in the *CYB,* then the format described previously can be used.

Another helpful resource for doing lectionary-based *lectio divina* is In Touch with the Word, a series of books published by Saint Mary's Press. You can look up the date of any Sunday and find a summary of that Sunday's readings, a review of the overall theme of the readings, and a focusing object. Each Sunday also includes three sets of reflection questions (one for adults, one for teenagers, and one for children) and a closing prayer, poem, or quote.

In Touch with the Word, and other resources like it, makes it easy to use the *lectio divina* process to prepare for Sunday Mass in a classroom, in a youth group setting, in a family program setting, or at home alone. I suggest adapting the steps in the following way:

Step 1. *Lectio*

Choose the appropriate day from one of the In Touch with the Word books. Display the focusing object where everyone can easily see it. To set the stage for what is coming on Sunday, read the description of the three Scripture readings, as well as the theme paragraph. Pause, and then have someone read the bulleted reading from the Bible.

Step 2. *Meditatio*

Read the reflection questions provided. Invite everyone to share the answer to a question of their choice.

Step 3. *Oratio*

Read the closing prayer, poem, or quote. Invite others to add a sentence or phrase of their own out loud.

Step 4. *Contemplatio*

This step is always the same. Prayerful, peaceful, resting in the love and tenderness of God's presence, being still, and just knowing and enjoying God.

Step 5. *Actio*

This step is often, but not always, covered by one of the listed reflection questions. One option, if you use this variation on *lectio divina* weekly, is to have each person share one commitment for the following week.

This method can work very well in a parish-based family program. You might try having younger children stay with their parents, and the teens (middle schoolers and high schoolers) mix up and sit with other parents who are not their own. Once the process is over, the teens can return to their real family and talk about their experience over breakfast, dessert, or whatever is being served.

One-Two Step Lectio Divina

This variation combines steps 1 and 2. All you need to do this form of *lectio divina* is a Bible. Its very simplicity can to lead to profound sharing.

Steps 1 and 2. *Lectio* and *Meditatio*

Have someone in the group read the scriptural passage. Then invite everyone to identify and share one word from the passage that seems important to them. Have another person read the passage a second time. Then invite everyone to identify and share one phrase or sentence from the passage that has special meaning for them. (The phrase need not contain a word previously identified.) In both cases ask them to share just the word or the phrase, not why it struck them as important.

Finally, invite another person to read the passage a third time. Then invite everyone to share in their own words what they think they most need to learn or consider from this passage.

Step 3. *Oratio*
Invite everyone to spontaneous prayer.

Step 4. *Contemplatio*
Again, this step is always the same. Be still and just know and enjoy God.

Step 5. *Actio*
Invite each member of the group to decide what he or she needs to do and to share some part of that plan with the others.

Group Creativity Lectio Divina

This variation requires preparation. Before the group gathers, identify the Scripture you will use and notify your group members in advance to read it before you gather. If you can, also give them the step 2 questions from the handout to reflect on. Finally, ask them to find or create something that expresses their meditation on the passage to bring to your class, meeting, or retreat. Some possible expressions are listed below:

- a poem
- a photograph
- a story
- a comic strip
- a newspaper article
- a drawing
- a clay sculpture
- a painting
- a prayer
- a symbolic object

- a song
- a dance

If you are doing this variation at a retreat, supply time and materials in order to facilitate the creation of these different forms of expression.

Instruct everyone in the group to bring the item they found or created to the group's meeting. Once you gather, go through the following steps.

Step 1. *Lectio*

Have one person read aloud the Scripture passage. Then have someone else read it again.

Step 2. *Meditatio*

Have everyone in the group share their finding or creation, along with their story of how it brings out the meaning of the Scripture passage.

Step 3. *Oratio*

Invite members of the group to share with God the feelings they experienced while seeing the Scripture passage through one another's eyes, as enhanced by the creations and findings everyone shared.

Step 4. *Contemplatio*

Again, this step is always the same. Be still and just know and enjoy God.

Step 5. *Actio*

Part of this conversation may be a discussion on how everyone's creations and findings might be shared with the rest of the faith community— whether that is the parish, the school, or a wider audience—as a service to broaden the experience others may have of a particular Scripture passage. You might suggest that the young people set up a display of the items. Or ask someone to photograph each item so that the young people can create a photo album to share with the faith community.

Options

This process could be used for a large gathering. A district or region could invite a small number of youth from each parish, along with their pastor. Each pastor could meet with four or five youth, and hear their stories and see their creations and findings. If each table is assigned a different Sunday Scripture, the resulting reflections could be collected and distributed to all pastors as youth-friendly homily helps.

Be Creative

I have offered just four variations on *lectio divina*. Use your imagination to come up with more. Anything that increases a young person's exposure to the Bible and enhances prayer life is worth exploring. Who knew that five Latin words would result in such divine reading!

Lisa-Marie Calderone-Stewart is a popular author and speaker with many years of experience in developing youth leadership. Among her best-sellers are *Faith Works for Senior High, Faith Works for Junior High,* and *In Touch with the Word,* a four-book series of lectionary reflections. Lisa-Marie is also the associate director of early-adolescent ministry for the Archdiocese of Milwaukee.

The Steps for *Lectio Divina:* Spiritual Reading

Step 1. *Lectio* (lex-ee-oh), "Reading"
Read the Scripture passage. Try reading it out loud. Try reading it several times. Let the words sink in deeply. Open your mind and heart to the meaning of the words.

Step 2. *Meditatio* (med-it-tots-ee-oh), "Meditation"
Reflect on the Scripture passage. Think deep thoughts. Ask yourself questions such as the following:
- What does this passage say to me?
- Who am I in this passage?
- What do I see? What do I hear?
- What do I think?
- Which character do I most relate to?
- What do I most need to learn from this?

Try taking notes on your answers to the questions. Try journaling about the insights gained with meditation.

Step 3. *Oratio* (or-ot-see-oh), "Prayer"
Move into the heart of the matter. Feel deep feelings. Consider the following questions as you respond to God:
- What do I want to communicate to God?
- What am I longing for in my relationship with God?
- What do I desire in my prayer life?
- What secrets of my heart are ready to be expressed? Is there joy? grief? fear? gratitude?

Express your intimate self to God in your own personal way.

Step 4. *Contemplatio* (con-tem-plot-see-oh), "Contemplation"
Simply rest in the presence of God. Be passive and just enjoy God. Settle into the tenderness of God's love.

Alternative Step 4 or Additional Step 5. *Actio* (ax-ee-oh), "Action"
Ask yourself the following questions in utter honesty:
- How is God challenging me?
- Is there a good thing God is calling me to do?
- Is there a harmful thing God wants me to stop doing?
- What is the next step I need to take?

Decide on a course of action (large or small). Make the commitment and follow through with your plan.

Holy Word Squares

Michael Theisen

In this chapter Michael Theisen shares a great technique for helping young people learn or review Bible facts. This game show format can be used in classrooms, in youth groups, and at retreats. After you have exhausted Michael's questions, substitute your own. This game is part of a collection of game show–based Bible games Michael is writing that will be published by Saint Mary's Press.

Who has not dreamed of winning big money as a television game show contestant? It was with this in mind that I created my first game show–based Bible game, So You Want to Be a Catholic Teenage Millionaire? for the 1999 National Catholic Youth Congress. It turned out to be such a success that I decided to create more Bible games based on a variety of television game shows. Now the teens in my parish keep asking for more.

Game show activities are successful not only because they are a lot of fun but also because they connect the young people by way of a common media experience. This connection creates a catechetical opportunity, so be sure to capitalize on it by taking a moment after each question to talk about why an answer is correct (I've supplied you with that information with the resource questions on pages 82–86). This particular game show activity is based on that perennial favorite *Hollywood Squares*.

Object of the Game

Like in the game ticktacktoe, contestants attempt to be the first player (or team) to get three x's or o's in a row. The three x's or o's can be horizontal, vertical, or diagonal. Players earn the right to get their x or o on a particular square by accurately deciding whether the guest star in that square has answered a Bible question correctly.

Players needed. one host (usually the group leader); nine guest stars (see the section entitled "Variations on the Game" if this many guest stars are not available); two contestants or two teams, each with a captain

Materials needed. poster board; a scissors; a marker; nine safety pins; eleven blank sheets of paper; ten copies of handout 1, "Holy Word Squares Questions"; masking tape; a coin; a Bible (optional); a prize (candy, a cross, a prayer card, or a book)

Set up. Recruit nine guest stars and give each one a name card with masking tape or a safety pin and a copy of the handout, "Holy Word Squares Questions." Meet with the guest stars privately. Let them know that every question the host will be asking is already printed on the handout you gave them. With each question are a correct answer and an incorrect answer. They may choose to respond with either one. Encourage them to be humorous with the contestants, even offering an initial response that is not listed on the handout. However, their final response must be one of the two choices on the handout.

Write a large x on each of nine sheets of paper. Turn the sheets over and write a large o on each one. Give one of these sheets to each guest star. Make two more signs, one marked with a large x and one marked with a large o. Tape these to the floor to mark where you want the contestants to stand.

Set up the game area as pictured below:

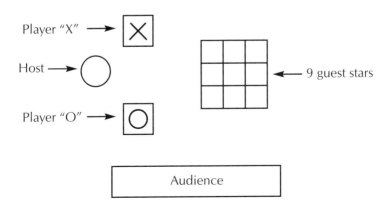

For added effect have the first three guest stars sit on the floor, the next three sit in chairs behind them, and the last three stand behind the people in the chairs. This gives the visual effect of a vertical square.

Rules of the Game

1. Invite the contestants and guest stars to stand in their designated spots, and introduce the guest stars.
2. Flip a coin to determine which contestant goes first. Be sure it is clear which contestant controls the *x*'s and which contestant controls the *o*'s.
3. Let the first contestant select a guest star. Read aloud for that star one of the questions about the Scriptures from the handout.
4. After the chosen guest star offers a final answer, direct the contestant to say whether the answer is true or false. Announce whether the contestant is correct.
5. If the contestant is correct, the guest star must hold up the mark the contestant is standing on (either an *x* or an *o*) for the remainder of the game. If the contestant answers *incorrectly,* the guest star holds up the opposing player's mark unless the mark would result in a win. *Note:* The opposing player cannot win the game because of a wrong answer.
7. After revealing the correct answer, take a moment to add the corresponding "Tidbit" statement from the handout. If your situation allows it, you may even wish to pause and have contestants and audience members look up the answer in the Bible. Keep in mind that the point of the game is for the young people to learn more about the Scriptures and not just to win.
8. If after all the squares have been played neither player has three in a row, the winner is the player with the most marks on the board.
9. Give a prize (candy, a cross, a prayer card, or a book) to the winning players.

Variations on the Game

Team play. After designating your guest stars, divide the remaining group into two teams. Select a captain for each team. That person's job is to be the official spokesperson for the team.

Guest stars. Recruit highly visible leaders in the parish or school—principals, pastors, parish council presidents, staff members, or local personalities—to be the guest stars. Reserve the "center square" for the best known of the personalities recruited. Young people can also serve as guest stars.

Free for all. If you do not have enough people to use guest stars, give each team a *Catholic Youth Bible* and direct the teams to be seated. Do *not* distribute the handout. Mark a ticktacktoe model on the floor or board and number the squares 1 through 9. Read a question aloud and let the teams use a Bible to find the answer. When someone thinks that they have the correct answer, they are to stand up and provide an answer immediately. If it is correct, they get to place their mark on any square they wish by calling out the number of the square they want their mark placed on. If their answer is incorrect, the opposing team gets to continue looking for the correct answer. If that team finds it correctly, it gets to place a mark. If it is incorrect, the square remains unmarked and another question is asked.

Numbered squares. If you do not have enough people to serve as guest stars, mark a ticktacktoe model on the floor or board and number the squares 1 through 9. Invite two contestants forward to play. Let the first contestant select a square, and then read aloud the question from handout 1 that corresponds to that square's number. Also read aloud one of the two responses. Instruct the contestant to answer true or false. If he or she is correct, award the square.

Invite the next contestant to select a new square from the remaining squares. Read aloud the corresponding question, and so on, until someone wins the game.

Michael Theisen is a popular author in adolescent religious education and youth ministry. He is one of the authors of *The Catholic Youth Bible* and is coauthor of *ScriptureWalk Senior High: Youth Themes,* both published by Saint Mary's Press. He also wrote five courses and the youth ministry manual in the Horizons Program. Michael serves as the coordinator of youth ministry for the Diocese of Rochester, New York.

Holy Word Squares Questions

Question 1. The first five books of the bible are also known as what?

Correct answer. the Pentateuch

Incorrect answer. the historical books

Tidbit. Pentateuch means "five-part writing." The Jewish faith also refers to these books as the Torah, which means "teaching" or "instruction."

Question 2. The story of Moses is found in which book of the Bible?

Correct answer. Exodus

Incorrect answer. Genesis

Tidbit. Moses is the Hebrew who led God's people away from the slavery of Pharaoh and Egypt and to the Promised Land, Canaan.

Question 3. "Blessed are the poor in spirit, for theirs is the kingdom of heaven" is the first verse of which famous saying?

Correct answer. the Beatitudes

Incorrect answer. the Great Commission

Tidbit. The Beatitudes (Matthew 5:1–12 and Luke 6:20–26) are teachings that offer ways of thinking and behaving in the world. They began what is called the Sermon on the Mount, and Jesus used them to help teach the people what the Reign of God was about.

Question 4. Which of the following books of the Bible is an epistle: Revelation, Tobit, Acts, or Romans?

Correct answer. Romans

Incorrect answer. Revelation

Tidbit. Epistles are letters written to the early church after Jesus' Resurrection. Many were written by Saint Paul or his followers.

Question 5. Which was the first Gospel written?

Correct answer. Mark

Incorrect answer. Matthew

Tidbit. Matthew is the first Gospel listed in the Bible (written around A.D. 85), but Mark was actually the first, and shortest, to be written (A.D. 65–70).

Question 6. Of the following four books, select the one that is not part of the wisdom and poetry books of the Old Testament: Psalms, Esther, Job, Proverbs

Correct answer. Esther

Incorrect answer. Job

Tidbit. Esther is a part of the historical books.

Question 7. What three people did Jesus take with him to the mountain to witness the Transfiguration?

Correct answer. Peter, James, John

Incorrect answer. Matthew, Mark, and Luke

Tidbit. They witnessed Jesus' face shining like the sun and the appearance of Moses and Elijah. Moses' presence affirmed Jesus as the fulfillment of the law. Elijah's presence affirmed Jesus as the fulfillment of the prophecies (Matthew 17:1–13).

Question 8. Who were the three major prophets?

Correct answer. Isaiah, Jeremiah, and Ezekiel

Incorrect answer. Micah, Amos, and Hosea

Tidbit. They are considered the major prophets because their books are long.

Question 9. "A soft answer turns away wrath, / but a harsh word stirs up anger" is from which book of the Bible?

Correct answer. Proverbs (15:1)

Incorrect answer. Judges

Tidbit. The Book of Proverbs is often attributed to Solomon because of his legendary wisdom, but the actual author is unknown. Proverbs was written from 970 to 538 B.C.

Question 10. In John's Gospel what does Jesus do at the Last Supper that does not appear in the other Gospels?

Correct answer. Washes the feet of the disciples

Incorrect answer. Asks John to watch over his mother, Mary

Tidbit. The washing of the disciples' feet is the action we remember and celebrate on Holy Thursday each year, as a sign of the type of discipleship Jesus invites all Christians into.

Question 11. The word *gospel* means what?

Correct answer. Good News

Incorrect answer. follower of Christ

Tidbit. The authors of the Gospels wanted to share the big and important news of Jesus Christ with the world.

Question 12. Of the following four people, select the one who was not a prophet: Obadiah, Haggai, Sirach, Jonah

Correct answer. Sirach

Incorrect answer. Jonah

Tidbit. The Book of Sirach was written by a wise man named Jesus Ben Sira around 180 B.C. It outlines the superiority of Jewish wisdom over Greek wisdom and is therefore part of the wisdom books.

Question 13. What is the longest book in the Bible?

Correct answer. Psalms

Incorrect answer. Genesis

Tidbit. The Psalms contain 150 psalms divided into five categories: hymns of praise and thanksgiving, hymns of lament or petition, hymns of wisdom, liturgical psalms, and historical psalms.

Question 14. The literary form that uses a fictional story to make a point is called what?

Correct answer. a parable

Incorrect answer. a metaphor

Tidbit. Jesus often used parables, such as the parable of the prodigal son and the parable of the lost sheep, to teach about God's Reign.

Question 15. What was Paul's name before he encountered the vision of Jesus on the road to Damascus?

Correct answer. Saul of Tarsus

Incorrect answer. Cephas

Tidbit. Paul had a profound moment of conversion as he traveled to Damascus. As a result of his experience, he switched from despising Christians to being one of their greatest leaders and evangelizers.

Question 16. Who is considered Israel's greatest king?

Correct answer. David

Incorrect answer. Saul

Tidbit. David was the successor to Saul, and he established Jerusalem as the religious center of Israel, moving the ark of the covenant there and bringing Israel to its zenith as a nation.

Question 17. Who replaced Judas as the twelfth disciple after Judas hung himself?

Correct answer. Matthias

Incorrect answer. Barnabas

Tidbit. In Acts of the Apostles 1:12–26, Peter leads the disciples in prayer. Then lots are cast to determine which of two people, Joseph or Matthias, would take Judas's place. The lot fell on Matthias.

Question 18. Which Gospel tells the most stories from the time before Jesus' birth?

Correct answer. Luke

Incorrect answer. Matthew

Tidbit. Luke's Gospel, written about A.D. 80, was directed toward Gentile (non-Jewish) Christians and included many stories affirming the dignity of marginalized people such as women, Samaritans, and poor people. Luke's Gospel includes Mary's visitation by the angel Gabriel and her visit with her cousin Elizabeth.

Question 19. The Jordan River connects which two bodies of water?

Correct answer. the Sea of Galilee and the Dead Sea

Incorrect answer. the Mediterranean Sea and the Red Sea

Tidbit. The Jordan River, where John baptized Jesus, was an important source of water and livelihood for many people in the Holy Land.

Question 20. Moses first encountered God where?

Correct answer. in the burning bush

Incorrect answer. at the Red Sea

Tidbit. In Exodus 3:1–12, Moses was instructed by God's voice coming from a burning bush to take off his sandals because he was standing on holy ground (the presence of God).

Question 21. Who are considered the father and mother in faith of three major world religions: Judaism, Christianity, and Islam?

Correct answer. Abraham and Sarah

Incorrect answer. Moses and Miriam

Tidbit. Abraham and Sarah are considered the founders of what later became the people of Israel. Because Jesus was a Jew, Christians also consider them their religious ancestors. And Muslims consider themselves "children of Ishmael," who was the son of Abraham and Sarah's slave-girl, Hagar.

Question 22. What was the name of the place where Jesus was crucified?

Correct answer. Golgotha

Incorrect answer. Midian

Tidbit. Golgotha means "place of the skull" and was the common site for crucifixions. The Romans wanted everyone to see what happened to those who went against Rome's authority.

Question 23. Which Gospel was written last?

Correct answer. John

Incorrect answer. Luke

Tidbit. The Gospel of John was written from A.D. 90 to 100. It was addressed to Christians throughout the world, many of whom were being persecuted for their belief in Jesus.

Question 24. The Book of Revelation is what type of writing?

Correct answer. apocalyptic

Incorrect answer. an epistle

Tidbit. Revelation was written by a Jewish-Christian prophet named John around A.D. 92–96 and was addressed to Christian churches undergoing persecution by Rome. His writings criticized Roman leadership, so he wrote it in a "coded language" to avoid being arrested. Revelation was not written to foretell the future, as some have claimed.

Question 25. In the story of Adam and Eve, how was Eve formed?

Correct answer. from the rib of Adam

Incorrect answer. from mud and water

Tidbit. Genesis 2:21–23 says God put man into a deep sleep and formed woman from one of his ribs, with the man later remarking, "This at last is bone of my bones / and flesh of my flesh."

Appendix A

Glossary of Biblical Terms

apocalyptic. Taken from a Greek word meaning "to uncover" or "to reveal." Refers to a style of biblical writing and imagery that focuses on mysterious revelations by angels and dreamlike glimpses into a world beyond. Often written during times of persecution with the intention of showing God's ultimate triumph over evil. This style is exemplified in the Book of Daniel and the Book of Revelation.

Apocrypha, apocryphal. Taken from a Greek word meaning "concealed" or "hidden." Christians use the term *apocryphal* to refer to ancient religious texts that do not have full canonical status, for example, the gospel of Thomas. Protestant Christians sometimes use Apocrypha to refer to the books and parts of books included in the Old Testament of Catholic Bibles but excluded from Protestant Bibles.

Bible. From the Latin and Greek word meaning "books." It is used most commonly to describe the sacred texts of the Christian churches. The Jewish community refers to its sacred texts—which are also the Christian Bible's Old Testament—as the Hebrew Bible.

biblical criticism. This is an umbrella term for a number of exegetical methods (*see* exegesis) used in the scholarly study of the Bible. Some of the specific methods are called textual criticism, historical criticism, literary criticism, form criticism, and canonical criticism. The word *criticism* is derived from the Greek word meaning "to judge" or "to discern."

canon. Derived from a Greek word meaning "rule" or "standard." Refers to a list of sacred writings or texts that are considered authoritative, recognized as an official body of writing by a particular religious community.

codex. One of two formats in which ancient manuscripts were written (the other being the scroll). The codex is leaf-book made of papyrus or parchment. Christians used this format to differentiate their sacred texts from the scrolls used in Jewish communities.

deuterocanonical. The first part of this word is from the Greek word *deutero,* which means "second" or "later." Used by Catholics to refer to those books or parts of books of the Old Testament that are included in Catholic versions of the Bible but not in Protestant Bibles.

eisegesis. Christians use eisegesis to refer to the risky practice of reading one's own ideas or biases into the meaning of biblical text. Compare to exegesis.

epistles. From the Greek word for *letter.* Refers to the New Testament letters written by various leaders to the early Christian communities.

exegesis. From a Greek word meaning "to interpret." Refers to the formal study of the biblical text, examining its origins, authorship, context, audience, language, literary form, and so on. *See also* biblical criticism.

Gospel. The English translation of the Greek word *evangelion,* which means "good news." Refers to the Reign of God preached by Jesus.

the Gospels. The four New Testament books of Matthew, Mark, Luke, and John, which both tell and interpret the story of Jesus' life and teachings.

hermeneutics. From the Greek word meaning "interpretation." When used by biblical theologians, it refers to a field of study that deals with the rules and procedures for correctly interpreting and defining the meaning of the Scriptures.

historical books. These sixteen Old Testament books recount the period of Israel's history from about 1250 to 100 B.C. They are not strict historical accounts but rather function as theological reflections on God's relationship with the Israelites.

New Testament. The twenty-seven books of the Bible written in apostolic times, that is, the decades following Jesus' death and Resurrection. The central themes of these books are the life and teachings of Jesus Christ and the beginnings of the Christian church.

Old Testament. The first forty-six books of the Bible. The Old Testament contains a variety of writings that tell the story of God's relationship with the Chosen People of Israel. Because the Old Testament is also the Hebrew Scriptures, Christians share this part of their Bible with Jews. Christians believe that the Old Testament is intimately connected to the New Testament because it prepares the way for the appearance of Christ as savior of the world.

Pentateuch. The first five books of the Bible, traditionally called the law of Moses. The books of the Pentateuch introduce many important people and themes necessary for understanding other parts of the Bible.

prophetic books. Eighteen Old Testament books that communicate the message of the prophets of Israel. The prophets spoke for God, warning the people against idolatry, calling them to act justly, and promising God's love and mercy in times of trial.

the Scriptures. From the Latin word meaning "writings." Used as another name for a body of sacred texts. Synonymous with the Bible.

Septuagint. From the Greek word for "seventy." Refers to a comprehensive translation of the Hebrew Scriptures into Greek that was begun in the third century B.C. by approximately seventy scholars. In study Bibles it is often abbreviated with the Roman numeral for seventy, LXX. Used as the basis for determining the books of the Old Testament in Catholic Bibles.

synoptic Gospels. From the Greek word meaning "seeing together." Refers to the three Gospels of Matthew, Mark, and Luke, which present a similar outline of the ministry of Jesus. It is widely believed that the authors of Matthew and Luke borrowed from Mark, as well as other sources.

Vulgate. From the Latin word meaning "common text." Refers to the authorized Latin translation of the Bible brought together by Saint Jerome in the late fourth century A.D. The Vulgate became the primary translation of the Bible for many centuries.

wisdom books. These seven Old Testament books are defined as much by their poetic form as by their content. They cover a variety of topics: psalms praising God, proverbs on how to live wisely and virtuously, and reflections on the meaning of life and human suffering.

Appendix B

A Basic Bible Resource Library

The following list includes books recommended as excellent foundational resources in building a biblical reference library:

Achtemeier, Paul J., ed. *The HarperCollins Bible Dictionary.* San Francisco: HarperSanFrancisco, 1996. With over thirty-seven hundred entries, a complete Bible dictionary for researching the people, places, events, and ideas of biblical times.

Bergant, Dianne, and Robert J. Karris, gen. eds. *The Collegeville Bible Commentary.* Collegeville, MN: Liturgical Press, 1989. Without being overly academic, this single volume has background information and interpretation on every book of the Bible.

Hiesberger, Jean Marie, ed. *The Catholic Bible: Personal Study Edition.* New York: Oxford University Press, 1995. Includes five hundred pages of excellent, easy-to-understand background on each book of the Bible; New American Bible translation.

Kohlenberger, John R., III, ed. *The Concise Concordance to the New Revised Standard Version.* New York: Oxford University Press, 1993. A concordance lists all the important words in the Bible and the verses in which they are used, making it possible to find passages and study particular themes.

Libreria Editrice Vaticana. *Catechism of the Catholic Church.* 2nd edition. Trans. United States Catholic Conference (USCC). Washington, DC: USCC, 1997. The *Catechism* has a complete index of Bible citations.

Ralph, Margaret Nutting. *"And God Said What?" An Introduction to Biblical Literary Forms for Bible Lovers.* New York: Paulist Press, 1986. This wonderful book answers in clear language the questions people commonly have about biblical interpretation.

Singer-Towns, Brian, gen. ed. *The Catholic Youth Bible.* Winona, MN: Saint Mary's Press, 1999. Filled with helpful introductions, articles, and study helps, this Bible is an excellent resource for youth and adults alike.

Witherup, Ronald D. *The Bible Companion: A Handbook for Beginners.* New York: Crossroad, 1998. A helpful, brief introduction to reading the Bible, with short overviews of all the biblical books.

An Expanded Bible Resource Library

As your biblical reference library grows, the following books will expand your ability to use and understand the Bible:

Brown, Raymond E. *An Introduction to the New Testament.* New York: Doubleday, 1997.

———. *Responses to 101 Questions on the Bible.* New York: Paulist Press, 1990.

Brown, Raymond E., Joseph A. Fitzmyer, and Roland E. Murphy, eds. *The New Jerome Biblical Commentary.* Englewood Cliffs, NJ: Prentice-Hall, 1990.

Brueggemann, Walter. *The Bible Makes Sense.* Rev. ed. Winona, MN: Saint Mary's Press, 1997.

Charpentier, Etienne. *How to Read the Old Testament.* New York: Crossroad, 1982.

Gardner, Joseph L., ed. *Reader's Digest Atlas of the Bible: An Illustrated Guide to the Holy Land.* Pleasantville, NY: Reader's Digest Association, 1981.

———, ed. *Reader's Digest Who's Who in the Bible: An Illustrated Biographical Dictionary.* Pleasantville, NY: Reader's Digest Association, 1994.

Hollyday, Joyce. *Clothed with the Sun: Biblical Women, Social Justice, and Us.* Louisville, KY: Westminster/John Knox Press, 1994.

Newland, Mary Reed. *A Popular Guide Through the Old Testament.* Winona, MN: Saint Mary's Press, 1999.

Ralph, Margaret Nutting. *The Bible and the End of the World: Should We Be Afraid?* New York: Paulist Press, 1997.

———. *Discovering Old Testament Origins: The Books of Genesis, Exodus, and Samuel.* New York: Paulist Press, 1992.

———. *Discovering Prophecy and Wisdom: The Books of Isaiah, Job, Proverbs, and Psalms.* New York: Paulist Press, 1993.

———. *Discovering the Gospels: Four Accounts of the Good News*. New York: Paulist Press, 1990.

Rohr, Richard, and Joseph Martos. *The Great Themes of Scripture: New Testament*. Cincinnati: St. Anthony Messenger Press, 1988.

———. *The Great Themes of Scripture: Old Testament*. Cincinnati: St. Anthony Messenger Press, 1987.

Scripture from Scratch. Cincinnati: St. Anthony Messenger Press. For more information about this four-page monthly periodical covering topics on the Scriptures, and a list of available articles, call 800-488-0488.

Vatican Council II. *Dogmatic Constitution on Divine Revelation (Dei Verbum)*. Council document, 18 November 1965.

Zanzig, Thomas. *Jesus of History, Christ of Faith*. Winona, MN: Saint Mary's Press, 1999.

Bible Resources for Ministry with Teenagers

Ayer, Jane E. *Guided Meditations on Discipleship: Readiness, Faithfulness, Conviction, Transformation*. Winona, MN: Saint Mary's Press, 1999. CDs and cassette recordings of the guided meditations are also available.

———. *Guided Meditations on God's Justice and Compassion: Accountability, Judgment, Acknowledgment, Selfishness*. Winona, MN: Saint Mary's Press, 2000. CDs and cassette recordings of the guided meditations are also available.

———. *Guided Meditations on Images of God: Mother, Potter, Compassion, Love*. Winona, MN: Saint Mary's Press, 1999. CDs and cassette recordings of the guided meditations are also available.

———. *Guided Meditations on the Paschal Mystery: Consequences, Idolatry, Revelation, Reconciliation*. Winona, MN: Saint Mary's Press, 1999. CDs and cassette recordings of the guided meditations are also available.

Bradbury-Haehl, Nora. *ScriptureWalk Senior High: Discipleship*. Winona, MN: Saint Mary's Press, 2000.

Calderone-Stewart, Lisa-Marie. *In Touch with the Word: Lectionary-Based Prayer Reflections*. Winona, MN: Saint Mary's Press. Published in four separate volumes with the subtitles *Advent, Christmas, Lent, and Easter* (1996), *Cycle A for Ordinary Time* (1998), *Cycle B for Ordinary Time* (1999), and *Cycle C for Ordinary Time* (1997).

———. *Know It! Pray It! Live It! A Family Guide to "The Catholic Youth Bible."* Winona, MN: Saint Mary's Press, 2000.

Drivdahl, Cheryl Miller. *"We Are Fire!" Resource Manual: Discipleship Activities and Prayer Experiences for Teens*. Winona, MN: Saint Mary's Press, 2000.

Haas, David. *Prayers Before an Awesome God: The Psalms for Teenagers*. Winona, MN: Saint Mary's Press, 1998.

Hakowski, Maryann. *ScriptureWalk Junior High: Bible Themes*. Winona, MN: Saint Mary's Press, 1999.

———. *Sharing the Sunday Scriptures with Youth*. Winona, MN: Saint Mary's Press. Published in three separate volumes with the subtitles *Cycle A* (1998), *Cycle B* (1996), and *Cycle C* (1997).

Koch, Carl, ed. *You Give Me the Sun: Biblical Prayers by Teens*. Winona, MN: Saint Mary's Press, 2000.

Krawczuk, Marge, ed. *Among Us! Scripture-Based Youth Ministry*. Dubuque, IA: Brown-Roa, 1995. A series of Bible studies with nine volumes: *Jesus' Ministry, Revelation, 1 Corinthians, Gospel Miracles, Gospel Parables, Gospel of Mark, Romans, 1 John and Galatians,* and *Sermon on the Mount*.

O'Connell-Roussell, Sheila, and Terri Vorndran Nichols. *Lectionary-Based Gospel Dramas for Advent, Christmas, and Epiphany*. Winona, MN: Saint Mary's Press, 1997.

———. *Lectionary-Based Gospel Dramas for Lent and the Easter Triduum*. Winona, MN: Saint Mary's Press, 1999.

Singer-Towns, Brian. *The Bible: Power and Promise*. Winona, MN: Saint Mary's Press, 1997. An active-learning minicourse from the Horizons Program, a senior high parish religious education series.

———. *Paul: The Man and the Message*. Winona, MN: Saint Mary's Press, 1997.

Theisen, Michael, and Nora Bradbury-Haehl. *ScriptureWalk Senior High: Youth Themes*. Winona, MN: Saint Mary's Press, 1999.

Audiovisual and Interactive Recommendations

The Bible Library for Catholics (Liguori Publications, 1996): CD-ROM for Windows and DOS, $99.95.

This is a great reference tool that makes it easy to look up passages, compare translations, and copy Bible text into another document for creating prayer services. It contains three complete Catholic translations of the Bible plus valuable study aids.

Available from Liguori Publications, One Liguori Drive, Liguori, MO 63057-9999; phone 314-464-2500; Web site *www.liguori.org.*

Bible timeline (Crossways International, 1997): wall chart, $14.50; transparency, $8.75; laminated foldout version, $3.75; the booklet *The Bible's Big Story: Our Story,* with a copy of the timeline inside, $9.00.

A good, accurate Bible timeline.

Available from Crossways International, 7930 Computer Avenue South, Minneapolis, MN 55435-5415; phone 800-257-7308 or 612-832-5454; fax 612-832-5553; Web site *www.crossways.org.*

The Blood of the Martyrs, volume 1 of the Passion of the Saints series (The Learning Channel, 1996): 50-minute videotape, $19.99.

Beginning with Stephen, the first Christian martyr, viewers see the great sacrifices men and women made for their faith throughout the ages. From the familiar stories of Joan of Arc and Thomas Becket to little-known tales of martyrs such as the twentieth-century priest Maximillian Kolbe, they behold how good triumphs over evil, time and time again.

Available from Discovery Channel Video, 700 Wisconsin Avenue, Bethesda, MD 20814; phone 301-986-0444 or 800-889-9950; fax 301-986-4826; Web site *www.discovery.com.* Also available from Gateway Films/Vision Video, P.O. Box 540, Worcester, PA 19490; phone 610-584-3500; Web site *www.gatewayfilms.com.*

An Empire Conquered (Marca-Relli Productions, 1991): 52-minute videotape with study guide, $19.99.

This moving docudrama filmed in Rome brings to life the intriguing days of the early Christians when followers of Christ were cruelly persecuted and martyred for their beliefs.

Available from Gateway Films/Vision Video (see *The Blood of the Martyrs* above).

The Gospel of Luke series (Genesis Project, 1979): set of four videotapes, 50 to 75 minutes each; $59.95 for the set.

Teachers may find this version of the Gospel of Luke more advantageous for Scripture study because the biblical text is narrated word for word over well-done re-enactments. This portrayal of Jesus is about as convincing and inspiring as one could imagine. The set of four videos divides the Gospel of

Luke into four parts—*Christmas, Early Ministry, Parables,* and *Easter*—with each part containing more than its title suggests.

Available from Rated G Films, a distributor for Bridgestone Multimedia Group, 300 North McKemy Avenue, Chandler, AZ 85226; phone 800-523-0988; Web site *www.bridgestonemultimedia.com.*

Jesus and His Times series (Reader's Digest Association, 1991): set of three 60-minute videotapes; $44.85 for the set, $14.95 for each video.

This series on Jesus reflects impressive biblical scholarship as well as superior writing, photography, music, acting, and production values. The titles in the series are *The Story Begins,* which covers the time around Jesus' birth to his visit to the Temple at age twelve; *Among the People,* which relates the ministry of Jesus from his baptism to his time of preaching and healing in Galilee; and *The Final Days,* which follows Jesus into Jerusalem and to his death and Resurrection.

Available from Saint Mary's Press, 702 Terrace Heights, Winona, MN 55987-1320; phone 800-533-8095; Web site *www.smp.org.*

Jesus of Nazareth (1992): 390-minute (6 $\frac{1}{2}$-hour) film, $59.95.

This is a classic feature-length film directed by Franco Zeffirelli, packaged in a three-video set.

Available for rental at video stores or for purchase from Rated G Films, a distributor for Bridgestone Multimedia Group (see the Gospel of Luke series above).

Judaism: The Religion of a People (Delphi Productions, 1994): 24-minute videotape with discussion guide, $195.00.

This documentary presents an overview of the practices, beliefs, rituals, and history of Judaism.

Available from AGC/United Learning, 1560 Sherman Avenue, Suite 100, Evanston, IL 60201; phone 800-323-9084; Web site *www. unitedlearning.com.*

Out of the Tombs (American Bible Society): CD-ROM for Windows, $29.95.

Inspired by Mark's story of the healing of the Gerasene demoniac, this award-winning computer program includes videos, music, maps, and interactive features.

Available from the American Bible Society, 1865 Broadway, New York, NY 10023-7505; phone 212-408-1200; Web site *www.americanbible.org.*

The Passover Celebration: A Haggadah for the Seder (Liturgy Training Publications, 1980): pamphlet, $2.95; 30-minute companion audiocassette, titled *Songs for the Seder Meal,* $5.95.

Available from Liturgy Training Publications, 1800 North Hermitage Avenue, Chicago, IL 60622-1101; phone 800-933-1800; Web site *www.ltp.org.*

Peter and Paul (MCA Home Video, 1981): 194-minute videotape with study guide, $39.99.

This video chronicles the ministries of Paul and Peter until their deaths in Rome.

Available from Gateway Films/Vision Video (see *The Blood of the Martyrs* above).

'Shua: The Human Jesus (ACTA Publications, 1987): 60-minute videotape with sixteen-page discussion guide, $39.95; book version, $8.95.

This unusual, intriguing videotape was created by Fr. William Burke, a master storyteller. To convey the humanity of Jesus, Burke has invented a boyhood friend of Jesus', who calls Jesus 'Shua. This character, played by Burke in contemporary dress, tells stories of his childhood, adolescence, and young adulthood with 'Shua in Galilee.

Available from ACTA Publications, 4848 North Clark Street, Chicago, IL 60640; phone 800-397-2282.

Voyage Through the Bible: New Testament, and *Voyage Through the Bible: Old Testament* (Jones Digital Century, 1995): CD-ROMs for both IBM-compatible and Macintosh computers, $39.95 each.

Actor Charlton Heston is the host for these remarkable interactive, multimedia journeys featuring key stories from the Bible. The CD-ROMs combine video of historical sites, three-dimensional animation, interactive maps and timelines, and more.

Available from JEC Knowledge Store; phone 888-757-8673; Web site *www.jec.edu.*

We Are Fire: Companion Songs for "The Catholic Youth Bible" (Comet Records, 1999): audio CD, $15.95.

A variety of Catholic musicians—both contemporary and liturgical—gathered to create this CD of original songs that parallel the major themes in *The Catholic Youth Bible,* which is published by Saint Mary's Press.

Available by calling 800-759-5805 or logging on to the Web site *www.davidkauffman.com,* and from Saint Mary's Press (see *Jesus and His Times* above).